MW01292342

The Culture of Incompetence

The Mind-Set That Destroys Inner-City Schools

John Cartaina

iUniverse, Inc.
New York   Bloomington

The Culture of Incompetence
The Mind-Set That Destroys Inner-City Schools

iUniverse books may be ordered through booksellers or by contacting:

*iUniverse
1663 Liberty Drive
Bloomington, IN 47403
www.iuniverse.com
1-800-Authors (1-800-288-4677)*

*Because of the dynamic nature of the Internet, any Web addresses or
links contained in this book may have changed since publication and
may no longer be valid. The views expressed in this work are solely those
of the author and do not necessarily reflect the views of the publisher,
and the publisher hereby disclaims any responsibility for them.*

*ISBN: 978-1-4401-6413-2 (pbk)
ISBN: 978-1-4401-6414-9 (ebook)*

Printed in the United States of America

iUniverse rev. date: 11/12/09

This book is dedicated to
my wife, Gloria, for all her love and support;
my wonderful children, Diane and John; my daughter-in-law, Helene;
God's gift, our grandchildren, Zoe and Jack;
and the children of Paterson, New Jersey.

CONTENTS

PREFACE

The nun told my mother I could stay if I didn't cry. I was four years and four months old, and that is my lasting image of day one in kindergarten. Just how tall was that nun? She looked like a mountain hovering over me. She scared me to death.

No child should ever feel afraid, lonely, or threatened in school. Today's classroom should be an oasis of safety and security in our chaotic world. Many years later as a teacher myself, I was always drawn to the students who seemed left behind or left out. Maybe I saw that scared kindergarten child in them. I empathized with the shy eighth grade girl from India who read novels all day in class. She did her assignments and was well behaved. In a tough inner-city classroom, she could easily have flown below the radar. But she never looked comfortable to me, and of course, that just couldn't be. Why was she shy, and why did she not want to mingle? I had to get beyond the novel that she used as a protective barrier. I would deliberately call on her, and she would push down the novel with an expression that said, "Can't you see I'm busy?" We eventually became such good friends that her mom invited me to their home. I never liked to see sad or isolated children in my class.

Teaching is a noble profession. It rests on a pledge between an adult and a child that is as sacred as the oath taken by doctors and ministers. A bad doctor kills one person at a time, but a bad teacher can kill the spirits of twenty children at a time. Teachers must inspire. They must exude dignity and integrity. If you don't want to be a role model, then find another profession. Teaching is a profession loaded with humanity. We have lost a lot of the opportunity for humanity in today's classroom of high-stakes state testing. Ironically, the emphasis on standardized testing can actually leave some children behind. We are supposed to be teaching children—not treating them like political pawns and overwhelming them with tests created by people who have not been in a classroom in years. We are their surrogate parents—not their testing coordinators. Quality instruction delivered by caring teachers can raise scores higher than the drill and kill strategies employed in some inner city schools.

Teaching can be exhilarating and frustrating at the same time. Only people who strive to touch the lives of children every day can understand the mountains of joy and the valleys of sadness that good teachers traverse.

This book is written for those people who see teaching as a mission to improve the lives of children who, through no fault of their own, do not receive the quality education that other children receive. It is for those concerned parents who drag themselves to school to visit a teacher after working the second or third shift in a factory. It is for those people who see education as a human and civil right whose quality should not be based on socioeconomic status or geographic location. It is for those teachers and administrators who bang their heads against the bureaucratic wall with occasional success.

I spent thirty-two years in the Paterson, New Jersey, school district. It is a poor, urban community in that very dense area of New Jersey between Newark and New York City. It has always been a port of entry city where Irish, Italian, Jewish, and other ethnic groups raised their children to become part of the American Dream. Today the groups are African-American, Latino, Arabic, and many others. The groups may be different, but the dreams are still alive, although housing and schools are older and the silk factories have become condos or crack houses.

I am proud of my time in the Paterson school district. I am prouder of the many parents, teachers, and administrators who strove to improve the lives of children. I love the children of that city—always have and always will. This book is in no way a condemnation of their efforts; rather, it is a salute to their dream and a call for help, support, and assistance.

Urban education today is either invisible to mainstream America or the pawn of the ten-second sound bite of politicians. Many Americans take the same view of urban education as they do of the homeless: out of sight, out of mind. They have segregated themselves in beautiful homes along the suburban sprawl and don't relate to the problems of the inner city. After all, if those people worked harder and didn't have so many children, their lives would be better.

No politician can get elected unless he is committed to improving education. We've had so many education presidents, governors, and senators that we could start a museum. They create standards, demand accountability, and blame parents for not preparing their children properly for school. Unfortunately, the funding for programs shuts down as soon as the camera lights go off. Politicians need to look in the mirror carefully. Do they truly want to improve the lives of children, or are their programs ineffective nonsense proposed just to get elected. Some politicians look at schools as employment opportunities for friends regardless of whether ability and a position really exist—"We'll just make up a title to suite the patronage." Some inner-city school districts should have red lights next to their signs—"We sell positions to any politician who can advance our agenda."

When I was a child a beer company's slogan consisted of three rings: purity, body, and flavor. Today, three rings deny inner-city children a quality education: incompetence, racism and politics. We accept the culture of incompetence in inner-city school districts because it reinforces our perceptions of minority children as nice but unable to learn as well as wealthy suburban children.

Racism is the elephant sitting in the corner of every classroom, administrator's office, and faculty room in the inner city. It permeates our relationships and clouds our judgment. Racism is the overt and covert use of race in decision-making. Racism can be found in the contractors who build inferior schools because "they" won't know any better.

Once, I organized a dinner for our eighth grade graduates. The menu was supposed to include soup. When I saw no soup on the table, I questioned the owner, who nonchalantly said, "'they' don't eat soup."

Racism permeates the employment process in many inner-city school districts. We need to replace a black male principal with a black male principal. This school is predominately Latino, so we need a Latino principal. Racism exists when a minority parent refuses to support teachers because they are white and live in the suburbs; quality not color should determine parental support of teachers. Racism clouds the judgment of teachers who expect less and less of their students as the number of minority students increases. Racism clouds the judgment of some experts and community members who believe that white teachers can't understand and teach black children. It is the quality of the teacher not the color of his/her skin that matters. As we become more and more of a diverse society, racism bounces back and forth among many races and ethnicities.

Every person who directly or indirectly affects the education of inner-city children is a stakeholder in the future of our country. Our democracy can not thrive when only children living in "good" neighborhoods get quality education. Political and business leaders; education experts at the university, state, and district level; administrators and teachers; and parents can continue to accept incompetence, racism, and politics as the norm, or they can realize that those factors are an affront to what our country is supposed to stand for: equality of opportunity. The culture of incompetence is the antithesis to the noble words of the Declaration of Independence. If we ignore the message of our founding document, then this can not be the country our forefathers envisioned. This is a country of hope and promise. All stakeholders in the education of our children must make choices to perpetuate the legacy of the Declaration of Independence.

I write this book in anger and hope. I have strong opinions on how to improve the quality of education in inner-city schools, and I hope my suggestions help those stakeholders who really care. As I sometimes rant about the need for change, many diverse memories flood my consciousness. As I add them to the story, I hope those memories uplift the spirits of the stakeholders.

Finally, I write this book because it just isn't fair. We parade some inner-city children as success stories in front of the cameras and shout, "She made it. Why can't everyone else?" Sure, there are superhuman children who can survive any environment and succeed. Two of my favorite people in Paterson today are success stories who overcame every type of obstacle the streets could throw in their way. I love them and am proud of them. But do we expect superhuman efforts from all wealthy children in excellent schools? No. So why must a child born in poverty be superhuman to succeed? Why can't he just be a kid and get a good education regardless of where he was born? Why can't a twelve-year-old city kid just be a twelve-year-old kid?

God bless the administrators, teachers, parents, and students who strive for excellence in a climate of racism, politics, and incompetence.

THE CULTURE OF INCOMPETENCE

Oh Well, That's an Inner-city School

Incompetence is accepted as the norm in poorly-run, inner-city schools. "Oh well, that's Paterson, Chicago, or New York" is a common expression used by teachers and administrators throughout the cities of America. Expectations for success are low due to a history of failure. Failure breeds more and more failure. It feeds upon itself. We assume failure and never expect success.

Visualize an inner-city school with a majority of students from low socioeconomic and sometimes broken families. Some of the students are African-American, and others do not speak English at home. Is your vision similar to one of the Hollywood movies about schools in the inner city? Why is the *Lean on Me* movie our image rather than an image of students working productively? Some schools are blackboard jungles, but when we accept that image as the norm, we perpetuate the problem and produce more incompetent schools.

Low expectations are compounded by our culture's historic confusion about race and poverty. Are poor people lazy, and do they really want to be poor? Can black children really learn as well as white children? Those questions have haunted our history, and they lay among the muck and silt of any river of change. Try to initiate change, and those sometimes dormant sediments rise from the bottom and cloud the chances of success.

If any initiative is introduced to improve the quality of education, some people simply say, "Be patient, this too shall pass." They are veterans of the inner-city wars, and they know the history of previous efforts. The effort to change is stymied by a failure to recognize the complexity and scope of the problem, which is centuries old and intertwined like a spider's web.

All problems must be attacked simultaneously. Sure, we need new school buildings, but if we don't improve the quality of teachers and administrators, what good will the new science lab be? Yes, we need smaller class sizes, but how much more successful will we be with twenty children from dysfunctional families instead of thirty? If a child is up all night because of an abusive mother and an absent father, will she learn more because there are fewer children in the classroom? Money alone will not solve the problem. Smaller class sizes alone will not solve the problem. Higher pay for teachers alone will not solve the problem. To break the cycle of unequal educational opportunity for inner-city children, we must break the backs of many problems simultaneously. We must attack racism among and between whites, blacks, and Hispanics. We must unchain the grip of sleazy politics from the halls of boards of education. If only one aspect of the problem is addressed, the winds of change are destroyed by the remaining overwhelming problems. Only then can we change the culture of failure and incompetence. Willy-nilly stopgap measures will always fail. The problems of inner-city schooling have historic implications, and there is no magic pill. If we attempt one solution without considering its impact on the other problems, the ignored weeds will strangle the seeds of change. Racism, incompetence, politics, and money must be addressed at the same time.

The core of the struggle to break the cycle of incompetence must include a belief system that all children can learn. Community leaders, administrators, teachers, students, and responsible government agencies must believe in the value and ability of poor children to learn, leave their egos at the entrances of the cities, and concentrate all their energies to redeem this national disgrace. All stakeholders are responsible for the quality of education in inner-city schools and therefore must make choices. Those choices can be responsible, or they could be to bury one's head in the sand and blame someone else for the problems. Let's be responsible for the future generations of American citizens.

The culture of incompetence incestuously breeds itself. It gives grossly inefficient teachers an excuse to continue working the same way. Why? Initiatives for change are either ill conceived or inadequately implemented or funded. So when they fail, incompetent teachers can smugly say, "I told you so." They continue to teach poorly, give everyone a passing grade for substandard work, and the community has a new pool of illiterate adults who help perpetuate a culture of crime in the city—"It's not me, it's the system"; "It's downtown's fault."

I witnessed so many new literacy programs and testing strategies that were heralded as the latest panacea. They were to be the best inventions since sliced bread. Most failed because they were poorly funded, were not supported by the staff or the community, or were devoured by other problems. The incompetent teacher simply bided his time, waiting for the program to fail. His incompetence was rewarded and perpetuated.

Every faculty room has a "Donut Dan" who sits in the corner and complains about parents, students, administrators, and the board of education. His constant complaining masks his incompetence. Every time incompetence is rewarded, Donut Dan wins and teaches another day. Every time we fail, we provide Dan with more ammo for his negativity. When an uncertified, incompetent administrator is appointed, Dan simply throws up his hands and says "it" is the new administrator's fault. When we accept inferior teaching as the norm, we make Dan look like a prophet. The acceptance of the culture of incompetence validates his existence. We justify his sitting in the corner and getting another donut stain on his tie. He is the mascot for the culture of incompetence. When we slay the dragon of incompetence, we will eliminate the necessity for his existence.

Dedicated teachers and administrators fight the pervasive culture of incompetence every day. Instead of rewarding those dedicated teachers, we give them more work: "Please be on an extra curriculum committee"; "Please take this extra troubled child"; "You're the one who can do this report well." How many years can we expect our excellent teachers to bang their heads against the wall? Thousands of young, quality teachers leave the poorer systems, disenchanted and disgusted. They are the people we should nurture and support not the winners in the system of incompetence. The future success of any school system lies in the hands of new, young, energetic teachers. We can't afford to lose them.

I lost an outstanding, young teacher who was not supported or appreciated at a large, comprehensive, inner-city high school. According to an administrator in the school, she wasn't very good. She was intelligent, bold, and displayed initiative to make changes. She was exactly what that administrator didn't want. He wanted someone who would say "Let's keep quiet, maintain the status quo, and just get to 3:00 PM." She moved on to an excellent suburban school where she immediately began teaching an advanced placement course. She wasn't good enough to teach in the failing school, but she was good enough to teach an honors class in an excellent school. Maybe if she had just kept her mouth shut, hadn't expected any change, she would have been evaluated glowingly. Part of the culture of incompetence is the acceptance of inferior teaching as the norm—"What the heck, these kids can't learn anyway."

When I hired that excellent teacher, I had also hired three other young, white women for the same department. Silly me, I hadn't checked their race or gender. When I came to visit the four of them, the security guard told me that some people in the school were guessing how long the four white women would stay. The implied message for most schools is always the same: "Give us some big men, preferably dark in color and skilled in Spanish. Only they can handle the kids. We don't care if they can teach; can they control 'them'?" We must ensure that great teachers are not like salmon swimming upstream, struggling to reach the top of the waterfall, and then too exhausted to continue.

Some poor teachers who stay become administrators. They learn the system well—keep your mouth shut, play the game, fill out the paperwork. They align themselves with the correct political group in power, and get appointed to positions in order to get out of the classroom. They run a school and are supposed to exhibit educational leadership. However, they are followers who wouldn't recognize quality instruction if it bit them on the behind. Some incompetent supervisors haven't left their offices "downtown" for so long, they would need a map to find the schools in their districts. No one would know they were alive if they didn't pass around a meaningless memo several times a year. They never cause "trouble," and remain in their jobs forever.

No supervisor or principal observed me during my first ten years of teaching. At that time, many inner-city districts were just looking for warm bodies to fill positions; they were not concerned about the quality of instruction, just with the body count. Some administrators raised the level of incompetence to an art form.

One administrator collected plan books and asked bilingual students to open the books to the last page with writing on it. Then the young girl or boy used the administrator's stamp on the current week's lesson plans. Why choose a bilingual student? Because she didn't know what she was reading. The administrator lasted for a long time in the district. She was politically connected, and when the school and parents finally got disgusted, the superintendent simply transferred her to another school. Her incompetence was rewarded.

Communities must hire visionary, charismatic superintendents for inner-city school districts. Children need superintendents who believe in their abilities to learn and succeed. People need to rally behind this leader and trust that he has a mission along with the ability and stamina to see it through. Arrogance should be checked at the board of education's door. The superintendent must be willing to work with the existing staff and community. He must be   humble enough to recognize that one person does not have all the answers. Troubled districts don't need bullies or egomaniacs with the my-way-or-the-highway mentality. A good superintendent does not want the job to pad his resume; he wants to make positive, sustainable change. Such a candidate is difficult to find for boards of education, because the pool of superintendents shrinks every year. However, if the political culture strangling districts is eliminated, more and more people will be attracted to the position. Currently, many superintendents are products of the political system where back-scratching and arranging quid pro quos replace vision and integrity.

A great superintendent or principal in a district that is predominately black or Hispanic doesn't have to be black or Hispanic. That's racism at its insidious worst. We need the late Dr. Martin Luther King, Jr., to remind boards of education that they need to hire based on the content of a man's character not the color of his skin. If the mentality is that a black school must have a black principal, then the community is cutting off its nose to spite its face. The small pool of qualified candidates for the position drastically shrinks when we limit the list of hires to one ethnic or racial group. Students need quality not color; they need to expand their horizons not limit them. Do communities that have that mentality really have the success of its children first and foremost on its agenda? Or do politics, racism, and hatred of anything white cloud its vision. It's about the children and no one or nothing else.

To break away from the culture of incompetence, we must take the appointment of teachers, administrators, and supervisors out of the hands of politicians. They do not have the right to dole out educational jobs as patronage to loyal supporters; I don't care how far back in our history this practice has been active. Because it has been done for so long doesn't make it right. It was wrong "back in the day," and it is wrong today. In addition to examining potential principals' resumes, trace their ties to local, state, or national politicians.

We must limit tenure for principals, administrators of schools, and all central office supervisors. These people affect the lives of too many children every day. They are not justices of the Supreme Court of the United States; they should not receive life appointments. Principals should be groomed in the same mold as superintendents. They should be instructional leaders and organized managers. They must believe and trust that all students can learn. Again, arrogance and ego need to be left at the schoolhouse door. Principals need to nurture and support teachers rather than conduct power play exercises. The message must be simple: "I demand quality instruction, will support sound educational projects, and will praise every positive act."

The principal must be a highly visible person in the school. I've been in schools where the main office counter is like a Berlin Wall. Administrators live happily on one side and believe that the school on the other side has no problems. Teachers and students have as much success seeing an administrator as East Germans had climbing over the wall during the Cold War.

Additionally, there should be written and oral tests for all administrative positions. The results of the tests should be made public, so everyone knows which candidate should get the next available opening. The written test must be created by a committee of trained professionals from the local district, university staff, and educational experts from the community. Oral tests should be conducted by a committee of teachers, administrators, and parents.

Unions and district officials should establish merit pay for teachers and administrators. The criteria could include, but should not be limited to, evaluations and observations, attendance, punctuality, parental contact, curricular and instructional initiatives, and extra curricular activities. Merit pay should be above and beyond normal contractual raises. If we want quality people, we must recognize their efforts and accomplishments.

We must fight to keep excellent teachers. Give new teachers buddies from within the school who can see them through difficult times. Professional development aimed at practical classroom experiences should be provided for all new teachers and should provide a support system for all teachers in their first three years of service. They should meet regularly with new teachers from other grades in the school and even from other schools in the district. They need to vent their frustrations, exult in their successes, and listen to fellow colleagues who are in a similar situation. New teachers should not feel alone and isolated in the classroom. They must feel that despite socioeconomics, decrepit housing, and unsafe streets, they have a chance to reach children who really need help.

I was very wet behind the ears as a first-year teacher. My enthusiasm was certainly tested by my lack of both preparation and supplies and an abundance of students. Many new teachers struggled along with me during that year. We went to a local bar/restaurant every Friday after school with some veteran teachers for food, drink, and conversation. Those venting sessions really helped me through that first difficult year. Like me, new teachers need support from all quarters.

University professors from local institutions should be hired to conduct some support sessions, because this places accountability at the appropriate levels. Education professors who prepared students for teaching must then support them in the field. If a professor's original message was accurate and effective, then encouragement, support, and refinement of the message are all that are needed.

What should we do about tenure for teachers? How do we get Donut Dan out of the profession? How do we ensure that quality teachers are not victims of incompetent, politically connected administrators? Tenure must be examined on a state and national level. There must be consistent, reasonable criteria to determine if a teacher deserves to be rehired. Tenure is granted after three years and one day of continuous teaching. A qualified administrator conducts several observations and evaluations each year for non-tenured teachers. If an administrator can't determine if a teacher is effective after three years, then something is wrong with the system of supervision or the administrator. Is the administrator given enough time to observe teachers properly, or is he called to boring, useless meetings at the central office?

Attainable, practical criteria to determine teacher effectiveness must be established on the state level at least, and each teacher must meet those criteria at regular intervals. A qualified teacher should not fear those criteria or retribution from incompetent administrators. If the standards are professional and accurate, it should be a "piece of cake" for the excellent teacher. The criteria should be a challenge and a goal for the average to good teacher and an exit sign for the incompetent teacher. Groups of qualified professionals with no political or personal agenda should be given the responsibility to develop those criteria.

Change can be difficult and disturbing. Inertia and acceptance are easy to maintain. However, we are Americans. We are from a nation founded on a philosophy that will always be an experiment and a challenge to accomplish. Not many countries are founded on the concept that all men are created equal; that we derive our rights from our creator and not from a governmental body.

The Declaration of Independence and the acceptance of incompetence in education as the norm are diametrically opposed to each other. Our founding document established the bar of equality of opportunity for all, regardless of race, religion, or wealth. We must not accept the belief that poor children can not learn as well as other Americans. When we follow that philosophy, we throw our very integrity as a nation into question.

Abraham Lincoln, the Civil War, and the ensuing amendments to the Constitution redefined our identity as a nation. That purpose must be redefined again as all Americans fight to break away from the culture that has framed inner-city schools far too long. All children must believe in their right to a quality education. Every American adult has a responsibility to address, vilify, and eradicate the culture of incompetence in and from our schools. Every child in America is our child. Let's make the right choices for our children. We must reward excellence, not incompetence.

The Teacher as a Person

You Believed in Us When We Didn't Believe in Ourselves

The role of teacher as a person is critical in inner-city schools. A teacher's humanity to students can be as important as the skills she learned in education classes; the teacher must connect to children in a personal way. All students can evaluate a teacher's humanity very quickly. If the teacher is not "the real deal," students will turn him off immediately. She's just another fake adult in their lives.

Generally, ineffective inner-city schools have many children from low socioeconomic neighborhoods. Some poor children have been ignored, abused, or neglected. If they are to learn, they must respect and relate to their teachers as people first. How many adults can inner-city children trust in their lives? One or both of their parents may be absent from the home. A tired grandmother may be the only force holding the family together; I met many warm-hearted grandmas who fought desperately to save grandchildren from the streets that had taken their own children.

Children watch television and notice the material comforts that other people their age enjoy. They know their books are outdated. They can see the ceilings that are chipping and falling in their classrooms. Some of their teachers never consider them important, but the teacher as a person may be the only adult the child can trust. A male teacher may have an even greater responsibility to be a role model. How many successful males are present in the lives of inner-city kids? There is a tremendous opportunity for all teachers to step up and make a difference in the lives of children at a time when children may not have anyone else. The connection must be real, genuine, and continuous. This point cannot be taken lightly at all.

There is a very easy measuring stick that can be used to judge how a teacher should treat students. She should treat them as she would want another teacher to treat her own biological children. She shouldn't ignore or isolate herself from her class and then complain about her own child's uncaring teachers. If she expects her own children to be treated with respect and dignity in school, then she needs to do the same for the children in her class. I remember some middle class teachers of various ethnic and racial backgrounds telling me that their own children were enjoying projects and activities in social studies in their schools. Yet when I visited those teachers' classes they taught children from poor neighborhoods with "dittos" and useless busywork. If interesting projects are good for their own children, then why aren't they good for students in their classes? Shame on them.

I particularly remember an eighth grade student of mine, who was an immigrant from Portugal. Because of family and language issues, she was turning sixteen in the eighth grade. She was a wonderful student and a pleasant young lady. When that young lady entered the class on her sixteenth birthday, she was greeted to the music of "Sixteen Candles," a cake, and her adoring classmates. I encouraged her to go to college, but she was concerned because she would be graduating from high school at twenty. She needed to help her family before thinking about college. Whatever successes or failures awaited her in the future, at least she knew on her sixteenth birthday that her classmates and teacher loved her as a person first and a student/peer second. She was recognized as a unique individual and treated as such.

When I was an administrator in a performing arts high school, I had the luxury of knowing many students by their first names. The school was very small, and students remained after school for rehearsals and performances. We developed overlapping schedules to free up classrooms for practices and electives. Each morning, I opened the school door at three different times and greeted less than one hundred students as they entered the building. I had the time and opportunity to talk to many of them about their homes, friends, and aspirations.

Talking to students on an equal, human level has a great impact on them. A teacher must really care about them if he asks questions about their lives. Their experiences must matter to that teacher. If he thinks they are worthy, maybe they are worthy. As a student said in her graduation address, "Teachers believed in us when we didn't believe in ourselves." Caring teachers helped her overcome a lack of self-esteem caused by a violent inner-city society that tried to rob her of her humanity and childhood. A teacher should make the attempt to connect to his students in a human, sincere way. It will be well worth it. He shouldn't be a poster child for incompetence; he should be a face of concern and caring.

How do teachers make a personal connection with their students? First and foremost, they must respect the children as equal human beings. Sure, the children do not have the knowledge, wisdom, or life experiences of the teacher. However, their equality is God-given and cemented in the philosophy of our Declaration of Independence. We often hear the complaint that children in school do not respect their elders, but I believe that respect should originate in the teacher. We are the experts in child psychology and teaching pedagogy. Shouldn't we recognize the importance of respect for humanity before the young, inexperienced child understands its importance? I hate when teachers tell students that they must earn the teacher's respect. How sanctimonious and egotistical is that? They are the children, and we are the professional adults. We must respect them as equals.

On the first day of most new school years, I wrote the words "respect" and "expect" on the blackboard. I respected them as fellow human beings, and that respect was guaranteed before I even knew them personally. Respect was a given from day one. I also expected a lot from day one, because I respected my students as wonderful human beings. My philosophy of education and practical classroom management strategies were built on those two words.

Excellent teachers have similar human characteristics regardless of where they teach. Those characteristics must include respect for children and enthusiasm for the profession. Excellent teachers obviously enjoy the company of children and have a limitless supply of energy. They are passionate and patient and have the courage to persevere. Excellent teachers are tolerant, compassionate leaders who exhibit a sense of humor. They must use the paradox of flexibility and firmness in their instruction and classroom management. They must ooze self-confidence and be able to motivate groups of people. Of course, I have probably described someone whose name is Jesus, Mohammed, or Moses. However, quality, functional school districts attract, demand, and hire people with some or most of those characteristics. Should inner-city districts settle for less just because the children are poor, abused, or neglected? There are inner-city teachers who display many of the traits mentioned above. Some maintain those traits throughout their careers. Some become disenchanted because they bang their heads against the culture of incompetence too often. We still must remember the crucial need for the teacher as a human being. Inner-city children need as many quality human beings to touch their lives as possible. Districts must attract, demand, hire, and support those teachers. To settle for less is to accept the culture of incompetence.

Poor school districts perpetuate incompetence by steering excellent teachers toward the few good schools in the district. Inferior teachers get transferred to the inferior schools. Do we accept inferior teachers because of our perceptions of students in the inferior schools: "Let's not waste an excellent teacher in that school. They can't learn anyway." We don't believe that poor children—many of whom are black and Hispanic—can learn. Teachers think, "Just keep moving them right along. When they are sixteen, seventeen, or eighteen, they will be someone else's problem." Sometimes I think large inner-city high schools are just holding cells for the city and state jails.

I vividly remember my first year as a teacher. One of my scariest moments was when the principal asked to see me after passing my classroom door. Of course, he never entered my room, but he still asked to see me. He had been the principal of the building for over twenty years and had a large, veteran, female staff. He brusquely said, "Cartaina, it looked like a good lesson you were teaching, but why did you take off your suit jacket?" Jump ahead thirty years to when I was a supervisor in the same district. Every time I visited that school, I took extra time walking around to stir up memories. One day, I attended an assembly program in the building. As all the classes streamed into the old auditorium, I was struck by the fact that most of the male teachers did not have a jacket or tie; some did not even have a collared shirt. If a teacher wants to dress like a night custodian, then grab a broom. If a person wants to be a teacher, then look, act, and talk like a professional.

The term "burnout" is overused and mistaken for incompetence. The flames of many burned-out teachers were never lit in the first place. Teachers should be passionate, excited, and alive for children who have little to cheer about. You can purchase e-tickets for a plane; I want "e-people" as my inner-city teachers. The *E*s stand for "enthusiasm," "energy," "enjoyment," and "expectations."

I had the privilege of working with great teachers during my two years as a traveling science teacher. They defined the term "e-teacher." One teacher conducted a staff development workshop during her last week before retirement. She was the most energetic, excited person in the room. Her flame never went out. We operated a traveling planetarium from school to school. We carefully led a small class and its teacher into the dark canvas cave to tell them famous constellation stories. I was the youngest of the four, and I was inspired by the dedication, enthusiasm for learning, and love of children the others had. Can you imagine how much the children enjoyed the presentations?

Teachers must have enthusiasm for their jobs and their professions. They should stop complaining. If things are so bad, they should change jobs or professions. Are teachers constantly complaining because they need a smoke screen to hide their incompetence? Is the best defense a good offense? Teachers should try not to be Donut Dan. They shouldn't do minimum work and complain constantly. They shouldn't add to the culture of incompetence. They should strive for excellence and become part of the solution.

Being an excellent teacher is a difficult job. Teachers are responsible for raising the intellectual, emotional, and social growth of twenty to thirty totally different children who come from totally different socioeconomic backgrounds. Why should students want to learn if their teacher doesn't want to be in the classroom with them? How can they have a positive outlook on their future when the person leading them is negative, disgusted, or depressed? Students easily read a teacher's body language and facial expressions.

Entering my last year as a public school employee, I had over three hundred sick days in the bank. Why did I keep so many days? How did I accumulate them? From my mother and father, I learned that you get up every morning and go to work. You don't make excuses. Just do the best you can. If I, as a teacher, took off ten to fifteen days per year just because I could, why should students come to school when they have to combat far greater hurdles than I have to to get to school?

Teachers in inner-city school districts must manifest leadership in their schools and classrooms at all times. They are in charge and must be take-charge people. By no means does that mean that they should be a dictator. I am thinking of the kind of leadership that is active and proactive in the students' personal and school lives. They must display self-confidence even though they are probably scared to death. A teacher needs to be firm but fair; these are two model adjectives for quality classroom management. Teachers should be motivators using many different methods. Some children are high maintenance and need constant encouragement. Other children are very independent and just need a wink of reassurance. Teachers must inspire them to believe that their potentials are limitless when they seem so limited. Teachers must believe in them when they don't believe in themselves. Teachers should take a stand and demonstrate their beliefs, not learn the system and how it works so they can move up the ladder. Teachers should learn how to beat the system for their students. They should learn which battles to fight and which to save for other days.

I worked for Dr. Morris Waldstein during my time as a science resource teacher. He was the greatest person, teacher, and administrator I have ever met. He told me that every teacher needs to find his or her niche. I'm sure he didn't mean a niche of comfort. Some teachers find a comfort zone, hide, and waste away. Other teachers decide that the classroom is not for them. They weasel their way through the system and find or create a position "downtown." Once there, they move irrelevant memos around central office to justify the fake position. Some become assistant superintendents. These are some of the people who make decisions that affect our children.

Teachers should challenge themselves as people and professionals to improve every year. The big picture may be depressing, but they should remain positive, refresh themselves often, and keep looking for the bright spots. They shouldn't beat themselves up after a bad day; they should get up off the mat and enjoy their students the next day. They should always look for new programs or strategies to improve their teaching skills. Enthusiasm for the profession will keep them fresh and alert. A wonderful woman in charge of staff development at the end of my teaching career introduced the district to the 4MAT model of teaching, which was based on the latest brain theories, and I thought it was great. I enjoyed the staff development and volunteered to be a trainer. I utilized the new strategies in my classroom, even though I had already been teaching for almost twenty-five years. It felt great being with other teachers who still had the flame to learn new methods to improve their quality of instruction. I gave up a week of my summer, but the recharging of my batteries was worth every minute.

Living in an inner-city community robs children of their childhood and humanity very early. There are reasons why twelve year olds can murder and show no remorse. They may have lost their souls to the street a long time before. Children absolutely need to see a human being in front of the class every day. That human being should be passionate, tolerant, understanding, and compassionate. Those adjectives are not synonyms for "pushover." The challenge for the teacher is to constantly display those human qualities and develop an orderly community of learners at the same time.

Some veteran teachers will advise new teachers not to get too personal with their needy children—"They will break your heart. You will not be able to function as a teacher if you constantly wear your heart on your sleeve." I totally disagree with that advice. A teacher's heart will be broken many times if she is an excellent teacher. Frustration lives with the great teacher daily. It's an occupational hazard. However, it's how she bounces back from frustration that will determine how long she can excel. She needs to clear her mind, do something good for herself, relax, and come back the next day ready to affect a child's life.

It is unfair to expect teachers to get up off the mat on many days and continue to be positive influences unless they receive the support of all appropriate stakeholders. We are not looking for martyrs to educate children. We are asking people with quality personality traits to work hard, because the rewards are great. However, teachers should not be scaling the mountain alone. There is no excuse for school leadership, the business community, the media, and the politicians not to provide the necessary support. If a person makes a choice to try to be an excellent teacher, then the entire American society must make the same choice.

There is no coincidence that "The Teacher as a Person" chapter is near the beginning of this book. Humanity is vital to the success of a teacher and to the lives of children, who—through no fault of their own—have no one to guide them. The teacher should be a real person, be a real teacher. He should help change the culture of his school. He shouldn't sell his soul as a teacher for laziness and disinterest. He needs to teach children not statistics, ethnicities, or colors. He shouldn't use children to further his personal agenda. He shouldn't perpetuate the culture of incompetence, rather he should be a leader and advocate for our most precious resource: children.

TEACHER-STUDENT RAPPORT:

The Heart of Classroom Management

You teach in an inner-city school? How can you control "those kids"? Aren't you afraid? You can't do anything for those kids; it's their parents' fault.

Those are just some of the questions and comments that I have heard, over the course of my career, whenever I told someone I taught in an inner-city school district. Of course, "controlling" children was never the reason I became a teacher. I was hoping to educate children not to control them. Control is not the goal of any teacher. It is the process to reach the goal of educating children.

How many times have I heard a principal tell me to visit the third floor of his school? "It's so quiet; I've got good teachers up there." "Is anyone learning?" should have been my response. Quiet and learning are not necessarily synonymous. Some of my class discussions in social studies on sensitive issues became very animated. Try talking about the eighth amendment and capital punishment in a class full of African-American males. A math teacher jokingly stopped me in the hallway with a complaint.

She had a great lesson planned for the day, but when my students entered her room still debating the death penalty, she was so intrigued by their passion that she let them continue. Social studies should be controversial and relevant, and excited children may not be misbehaving; they may be learning. Some administrators would have been better suited being wardens in jails. Control and silence is all that matters to them.

The teacher as a person must bring his humanity to the classroom every day. That humanity, as discussed previously, is integral to any personal or professional success. No classroom management system in an inner-city environment can succeed without quality teacher-student rapport. That relationship can not flourish unless the teacher consistently displays a humanity, which may be missing in the child's personal life.

Classroom management is crucial for educating children rather than just controlling them. It can be defined as the system of organized procedures necessary for a nurturing climate of learning. That system is created and implemented by caring, qualified teachers who have developed a warm, genuine relationship with their students. Classroom management is preventive and proactive; discipline is corrective. The better the classroom management, the less discipline a teacher needs. If teachers walk into school in the morning at the same time as the students and have poor or no lesson plans, they will need a lot of discipline. The more discipline a person needs, the more control becomes the main reason for her existence as a teacher.

I remember many teachers who had to run to the sign in book in the morning so they wouldn't be marked late.

Then they ran to their classes or out to the playground to meet their students. It took the teacher ten or fifteen minutes to get settled; all the while, the students sat with nothing worthwhile to do. Someone would enter the room, and the teacher would complain about how badly the students were behaving. She exclaims, "These students are not the same as they used to be." with a condescending tone and look.

Good classroom management incorporates both skill and humanity. Classroom management is a function of many factors. I would stress these essential components: teacher-student rapport, quality lesson plans, and preparation/organization.

I often used the phrase, "Respect a lot, Expect a lot," as the theme for my classroom management style. It was always plastered on one of my very inartistic bulletin boards in class. To me, it symbolized my philosophy about the relationship between teacher and students. The heart of classroom management is the relationship between the teacher and students. No list of rules, point systems, or games can compensate for the failure of teachers as human beings to develop a genuine rapport with the fellow human beings they will be working with for a year. The teacher must be genuine and proactive in the development of this relationship.

Elaborate and complicated point systems or games never work for effective classroom management. The Bluebirds have accumulated 10,000 points this week, but the Jaybirds are close behind with 9,900. If I raise my left hand instead of my right is that a demerit? I don't want to lose points for my team. Now what did the teacher just say about adding fractions? The point system becomes the focus of attention instead of the means to focus attention.

How does a new teacher develop a relationship with a group of children he has just met? He should be himself, be human. He should read, understand, and internalize the previous chapter of this book. If that chapter does not make sense to him, then he should choose another profession. It is a teacher's responsibility to treat his students like fellow human beings, equal to him in every way except the expertise of teaching and the experience of adulthood. Respect their humanity.

Inner-city children are often robbed of their childhood or forced to act tough or streetwise because of their environment. Many days they come to school and do all the silly things that any child would do in school. Other days those same children wear their street masks for defense to cover up the hurt and violence they felt the night before. Never forget that they are human beings first and foremost.

I chaperoned several three-night class trips to places like Washington DC and Boston. We always had a great time, and the children behaved magnificently. A group of thirty students and three teachers spent four days and three nights in the Virginia area. The bus broke down on our way home. Needless to say, we were all exhausted and didn't need the extra excitement. As the bus pulled up to our school at two or three in the morning, instead of early the evening before, I noticed that all the students were sleeping. The bus driver wanted to fully illuminate the bus. The children were all asleep, and many had a favorite stuffed animal, blanket, or some other sleeping prop from home. At that point, they all looked like teenage children. They were innocent creatures safe in their dreams. The anger and resentment they carried with them because of where they lived was replaced by the quiet of a good sleep. I gently touched each of the children to wake them up. It was one of the most precious moments of my career. I might have touched them to wake them, but they touched me with their innocence. Never forget they are human beings first and foremost.

Too often teachers in inner-city schools forget that their students are children. Sometimes students represent the teacher's "cause" to change the world, or they are lumped together as a "them," as almost inanimate objects that just don't want to learn. To politicians and their lackeys, students can become pawns in the crazy world of raising test scores.

They are children first before they are enrollment data, a tenth of an increase in a test score, or a member of a racial or ethnic group. I argued with a teacher once who insisted that a child is a Latina first and a child second. I could not believe the stupidity and cruelty of that belief. The child was merely a vehicle for that teacher to push her own political agenda and spread her hatred for white men in power.

There is very little that one can learn in a textbook about establishing classroom rapport; we must celebrate and respect the individuality of the child. This is definitely a case where the "science" of teaching must take a back row to the personal humanity of the teacher. The teacher must either love them, and want to be with them every day or get out. He shouldn't waste the children's time with any other excuse.

Children must know their teacher cares for them. There is no gray area in a teacher's relationship with students. Children can smell a phony just as easy as they can smell the bad pizza for lunch.

Who respects a student? It is the teacher who takes the time to listen to a child, even though the child tells the same story every Monday morning. It is the teacher who wants to know about their students' baby sisters, ill grandmas, and pets that get them into trouble. The teacher respects the student when she shows his parents respect when they visit the class. The child knows that his parent doesn't speak English well or is not dressed as nicely as other parents or maybe combs her hair in an uncool manner. The teacher will win the hearts and souls of her students by just showing respect to their family.

Teachers who water down the curriculum because "they" just won't get it have no respect for the right of all children to a quality education. Teachers who pander to inner-city students by setting expectations so low and excuses so high have no respect for them. We must respect and trust a student's ability to learn. That sounds like a simple statement, but the unspoken belief that "these kids can't learn as well as other children" permeates the culture of mediocrity, incompetence, and racism in inner-city schools.

However, school teachers are not miracle workers. If a student comes to kindergarten in an inner-city school already several years behind, then all stakeholders need to work together to fix the reasons why she is several years behind. We have the resources and intelligence to fix the problems; we just don't have the will and conviction to do so. It is easier to allow the problems to support and perpetuate our racist beliefs that "those kids" can't learn.

Teachers who respect every child's right and ability to learn and who develop high expectations for success must be the cornerstones of an effective, humane classroom management system. Use "respect" and "expect" as an umbrella to cover all rules in the classroom: "Because we respect each other, we don't swear or curse at each other." Teachers cannot accept crude, street language in the classroom. If they accept it, they sanction it. Do they sanction it because they do not believe the students can behave better?

As a student, I would expect to come to a safe, nurturing classroom each day; I would expect to find my teacher prepared, organized, and anxious to greet me. When I taught grades six and eight in middle school, we were still in the Stone Age, and students were placed in self-contained classes. Students only left the room for lunch and special subjects like gym, art, and music. Keep them under control. Classes moving through the halls had to be orderly so as to not disturb other classes. Instead of threatening the class, I told them I expected them to walk quietly because they respected both themselves and their teacher. I expected much of them, and they needed to respect themselves enough to walk like students with a purpose.

I like the word "choices" instead of "rules" for creating the expectations for class behavior. Students choose to respect each other, because that is the correct thing to do. They don't choose to respect each other because they are afraid of the teacher. The teacher must be firm but fair in implementing the respect and expect guidelines.

As the year progresses, the class can revisit the terms respect and expect. The students can actually gain ownership of classroom management by discussing and expanding the two terms. Empower the students to define and outline behaviors that exhibit respect and high expectations. This can grow into a plan of action for the class. Students will definitely follow a plan that they have helped create.

There are many non-instructional activities in the daily life of a classroom that can destroy the teaching process if not accomplished correctly. Collecting homework, going to the nurse or bathroom, raising one's hand, and passing out papers are just some of those activities that can cause chaos if not planned well in advance. Once the teacher-student rapport has been allowed to germinate and grow the teacher can proceed with the structure necessary for successful classroom instruction. Without the rapport in place, the above activities can only be accomplished through threats, screaming, or sheer cruelty.

All students want and need structure in the classroom. Students who come from broken homes and have little structure in their family life particularly need and want it. Teachers should develop structure and routines in those classroom management activities mentioned before that could doom instruction if mishandled.

The great fallacy in education is the belief that a teacher must be cruel and mean until Christmas and then lighten up a little. The teacher can develop firm but fair structures in the classroom and still be the human person mentioned in the previous chapter. A teacher does not need to be Hitler to succeed. Again, he may have a quiet class, but who is learning?

If teachers want a genuine rapport with their students to maintain quality classroom management, then those teachers must create an atmosphere of learning and purpose through respect and high expectations. Before reading a textbook on classroom management, a teacher should look into his heart and soul and his reason for becoming a teacher in the first place. If those reasons are sound, then he can build a successful classroom management system.

THE TWINKLE IN THE EYE

Learning the Skills of Teaching

Teaching is a very difficult job. We expect teachers to be knowledgeable in their subject matters and to love and understand children. In our diverse culture, we also expect them to be social workers and surrogate parents. It is the most difficult, yet most rewarding profession a person can choose. It is also a profession that chooses you, as I noticed quite frequently in the passion of student teachers.

Once people realize they have the heart to teach, how do we ensure that they will learn and use the skills of teaching? Teacher preparation and support must be a lifelong process that begins in the early stages of college life and continues through retirement. Teachers in the field must feel like they have a lifeline of support from education experts from the university level to central office personnel in their district to the community itself.

Training may begin as soon as an undergraduate student chooses education as a major at a certified college or university. Prospective teachers choose a core group of academic courses in subjects like language arts, math, science and social studies. Those courses must mirror the standards of syllabi from courses that majors in those subjects should master. There must never be a difference between a United States history course for history majors and one for education majors. How can someone teach the content if he doesn't master it? We expect children to meet world-class standards on state assessments, yet we produce education majors who have not received world-class training. Content for education majors must never be watered down.

When I was a supervisor of social studies, I was astonished at the transcripts of graduating college students looking for employment as teachers. Courses that I considered electives passed as core subject requirements. People were hired to teach world history who had never taken that course at the college level. Geography is a skill infused in all grades, yet some graduating seniors never had a geography class in college. Some colleges and universities have addressed the issue, creating specific core course selections. As I stated in the previous paragraph, the level and complexity of content for courses taken by education majors must be the same as courses taken by history, English, math, and science majors. Teachers must be historians, mathematicians, scientists, and linguists who also have the heart and skill to reach children. I absolutely do not believe in the phrase, "Those who can do, and those who can't teach." We owe our students the most qualified teachers possible rather than just people who "couldn't make it in the real world." If we are to change the negative climate of incompetence, we must staff our schools with great teachers who have warm hearts and are masters of content.

Many new teachers enter the profession as a second career. Thirty- or forty-year-old moms who have registered their youngest children in kindergarten now want to follow their dreams of becoming a teacher. Fathers who are tired of the rat race at work and want to be at home for their children at night change careers to become teachers.

I have had the privilege of working with many passionate people who made the life-altering decision to educate young children. They were nervous and sometimes unsure of themselves, but they amazed me with their determination to absorb every bit of advice I gave them. I have been humbled by their desires to change the lives of children. To this day, some of them still call or email me with questions and concerns. It has been one of the highlights of my career to work with such dedicated people. I framed a letter of thanks from one group, and I read it regularly to remind me of the hope for the future. They are definitely the type of people that the universities, communities, and districts should nurture for many years. They have made great personal choices for themselves and for the future of our society.

Many Americans are quick to point fingers at teachers as the cause of the failure of education in our inner-city schools. Most politicians can't use the word "teacher" in a sentence without using the word "accountability." Teachers must respect their students and treat them with dignity and humanity. But who respects teachers? Who treats teachers with respect and dignity? It is a bit hypocritical to ask teachers to act in a professional, humane manner when we don't treat teachers the same way.

All new teachers must feel connected to a university, a school mentor, and a district supervisor for at least the first few years of their careers. I have truly enjoyed observing and evaluating student teachers. But I believe the connection to the university professors should not end upon graduation or certification. That valuable relationship should continue for the first few years of the intern's teaching career. Think of the powerful connections that could be developed. A supervisor of student teachers could become one of their mentors until the novice teachers gain tenure. The university could choose regional sites to provide masters level education courses taught by the same mentors. The novice teachers could have weekly contact with the same education professors who taught them in college or supervised them in the field.

Colleges and school systems must become partners in the lifelong process of preparing and supporting teachers. Inner-city schools, especially, should open their doors to colleges to be used as laboratories for educational training. College classes in urban education should spend some of their time in the public school systems. Several class periods should be conducted right in the schools. College students should see the daily operations of the schools—victories and failures. When I was an undergraduate, the university actually had a high school on the campus. We observed our college professors teaching high school students and were able to discuss those classes in our next college session. Colleges and district training must mirror the real world. What better way than to have the professor teach in a real high school?

Once those new teachers become quality veterans, they can become mentors to new teachers. Both the mentors and new teachers should have a lifetime of support and training. We cannot afford to throw teachers into the deep water of their first classroom and then forget them. "Sink or swim" should be replaced with "swim and we'll be there to help you." We don't want Donut Dan to become a hero and mentor when he says, "Forget everything you learned in college, this is the real world."

One of the first people a new hire should meet is the supervisor or director of staff development. That district person is a valuable support person for the novice teacher. Just as the professor is the link to the university, the staff development supervisor is the link to subject supervisors, district office personnel, and all new opportunities for creative programs and strategies. The teachers should always feel like they are in a supportive cocoon. Then they will never free-fall after a bad day, because someone with a great deal of experience is there to catch them. That is the only way we can recruit and keep excellent new teachers. They must feel they are part of a great mission to improve instruction.

The supervisor of staff development has the responsibility of creating interesting, relevant training sessions for teachers. There have been new, exciting breakthroughs in brain theories regarding learning and behavior. New teachers need constant support with classroom management skills and conceptualizing quality lesson plans. A myriad of great topics should be addressed at training sessions for teachers. The skill of teaching always needs fine-tuning.

However, district teacher training sessions can be boring and useless. Incompetent district supervisors who don't make frequent connections with their staff often provide horrific training sessions. Since they don't spend the time getting to know their staff, they don't know the staff's needs. It is the same parallel with a teacher and a class of students. Teachers must know their students and make real, personal connections with them. Then they learn what and how their students need to learn. Supervisors who spend all day in their offices writing meaningless memos will create meaningless workshop sessions. They will pontificate about some topic totally alien to a teacher's real-life situation. The teachers sit in the sessions and count the minutes on the clock on the wall. Often these sessions make teachers realize what it must be like for a student in a boring class. What about the student who experiences chronic failure in traditional classroom settings? What hell we put our failing students through.

It was with that mentality that I attended a teacher training workshop in one of our very old, hot buildings on a spring day in the early seventies. I was sitting in an old one-piece wooden student desk hoping not to catch my pants on one of its many splinters. It was an afternoon session, so I had already taught four hours of class in the morning. The room was very warm, and I tried to look out through the dilapidated, stained windows for some sign of spring.

As I glanced away from the window, I noticed a tall elderly man with a full head of gray hair enter the room. He carried a small cardboard box that had, at one time, contained Girl Scout cookies. What caught my eye, however, were his eyes. He had a twinkle in his eyes like a small boy getting his first chemistry set. He was excited to be with us, and the smile on his face told us that he was having fun.

Dr. Morris Waldstein took a few pieces of electrical wire, sockets, bells, and batteries out of his box. It was playtime and show–and-tell all rolled into one. He began to demonstrate how science should be hands on and fun. I was amazed by the man's entire persona. How could I, as a young teacher, complain, when this veteran of many teaching wars was obviously having a ball playing science with us?

That day began a relationship that changed my professional life. He was the greatest man I ever met. He was as rare a teacher and supervisor as he was a great man. Academic brilliance and humility lived within the same person. He expected great things from students and teachers, yet he was extremely compassionate and kind. Our relationship lasted until his death several years later, and there wasn't one time that I was in his presence that I wasn't in awe of him. He had the ability to connect to his staff in a real, personal manner.

Dr. Waldstein was the science supervisor, and he asked me to participate in several districtwide projects. Students in my sixth grade class received weather equipment from Doc, and each morning, they measured indicators such as temperature, rainfall, barometric pressure, wind speed, and direction. Then we called Eastside High School with the recordings. No matter how many times I made a mistake, Doc was patient and kind. He explained cloud formations over and over until I could recognize them easily.

Doc wanted me to leave the classroom and join him as a traveling Mr. Wizard. Officially, I was a science resource teacher, but we were really his Boy Scouts. I say "we" because three sensational science teachers joined me: Vicki Madden, Josie Culmone, and Catharine Whitaker. We lived out of the trunks of our cars for one full year. My wife was actually a Girl Scout leader at the time, so I had wires, batteries, bells, and sockets in old Thin Mints boxes, animal specimens in Tagalong boxes, and so on. We traveled from school to school, performing demonstration lessons for teachers in front of their own classes. It was a hectic, busy year, but I would have walked through a wall for that man.

One of our favorite activities of the year was a portable planetarium. It was really a large inflatable canvas bag with a state of the art projector that displayed the constellations on its cave-like ceiling. We had so much fun telling stories about the constellations. Bootes is a constellation shaped like an ice cream cone. Of course, its flavor was heavenly hash. Orion and Leo roared through the heavens as we moved the sky across the seasons. Recycled air was pumped into the planetarium, but after several lessons per day, we were as groggy as a drunk walking out of a bar at 3 AM.

One of the first times we performed a lesson for students was on a stage in an elementary school. The four of us were very nervous, but the session went very well, and the students learned astronomy in a fun-filled hour. As we left the planetarium, we were horrified to see that Dr. Waldstein had been sitting in the first row of the auditorium listening to us. Would this great man think we had performed adequately? We walked off the stage, praying for his approval. When we reached him, there were tears in his eyes. Over and over again, he told us how proud he was of us. I have never had a private audience with the pope, but Doc's pride in us that day must be close to that feeling.

Dr. Morris Waldstein passed away as a result of asbestos cancer very soon after retiring. I hope to God that I have been some source of pride to him as he has sat in heaven with his torn cookie box of wires, bells, and batteries.

Where are the Morris Waldsteins today? How many administrators, supervisors, and teachers have the twinkle in their eyes? I believe there are thousands of dedicated teachers who recognize that the profession is more than an eight-to-three job; it is an opportunity to change a child's life. Sadly, too many dedicated teachers leave the profession within a few years. Often, the most incompetent teachers find a little niche of comfort and just waste away.

We must build a network of support for new teachers to sustain them throughout their careers. Every professional that the new teacher comes in contact with must be part of the support system. Think of the power of this network. Undergraduates, student teachers, new and veteran teachers, mentors, administrators, and district and university personnel must all work together to smash the status quo. The culture of incompetence is insidious, systemic, and pervasive just like the problems that attack inner-city schools. A new climate of professionalism, support, and enthusiasm must become the new culture, the new status quo. That new culture will support the heart and skills of new teachers. University officials and school district personnel must make practical choices to support and nourish new teachers so those teachers can do the same for their own students.

The Living School

Experienced Educators Can Determine If a School Is
Effective within an Hour of The First Visit

I do believe that experienced educators can identify an effective school in a matter of hours. The extent of the effectiveness may need more time, but obvious clues jump out at us as we walk down the halls of most schools. That's because a school is not a building; it is a living organism that performs a vital social function within the walls of a physical plant. It can be vibrant with the exhilarating sounds of students learning and growing, or it can be stifling with dysfunction and despair. A school develops the social, emotional, and academic lives of children, or it destroys natural curiosity and creates illiterate, dysfunctional citizens who depend on of participating in that society.

What are the obvious clues that tell us if a school is an effective institution? Walk into any inner-city high school. Are the hallways dark and foreboding? Are the bulletin boards and display cases bright, positive, and most of all, up-to-date? When the bell rings for the change of

classes, do the students move with a purpose? Do the security guards have to shepherd reluctant students to class and away from known hiding places for those who cut school? Go to the cafeteria during lunch. Does it resemble a jail with teachers, security, and maybe even police officers acting like guards? Do the students clean up after themselves, or must lunchroom monitors clean all the tables? Is there a buzz of happy students talking, or is there a rumble of discontent? Is it obvious that one small altercation will cause chaos?

While the students are in classes, walk down the halls. Look at the students' faces as you peek into the rooms. Do they seem engaged in the lessons? Are they active learners? Are the teachers facilitating and inspiring learning or simply chalking and talking and passing out meaningless dittos? Is there a positive energy in the class? Great administrators can feel the rapport between students and teachers as they observe classes. There are positive vibes in the room. All of the answers to the above questions can be found within an hour or two at most schools. If the answers are all negative, then the school acts like a different social institution: it is simply is a holding pen for the county jail. I've seen high school classroom doors that are metal and have tiny slits for light. What kind of building comes to mind?

A child enters school as a curious, impressionable creature, anxious to grow and learn. A living school can provide the nurturing environment for that child's growth. What is a living school? I'll define it with these words: hope, purpose, joy, and learning. It is an environment and a state of mind where adults and children believe in each other, work together, and grow together. Adults grow as much as the children in a living school. They both develop and feed off each other's enthusiasm. Children bring their innate curiosity, and adults bring life experiences. The symbiotic relationship nurtures everyone. It can be a place an inner-city child runs to in the morning to escape the chaos of life in the streets.

Departments of education attempt to lower the truancy rate in some schools. If the school itself is chaotic, then life at school mirrors life at home. Why should a child attend a chaotic school? He might as well "chill in the street." I'm amazed that the rate is not higher considering some of the dysfunctional schools I have seen.

Some of my favorite schools were definitely living organisms. Students and teachers were happy as they moved about the building. There were always pleasant hellos from administrators, teachers, and students. Every bit of wall space was covered with students' work.

One particular third- or fourth-grade class drew templates of the fifty states. Parents agreed to bake a small sheet cake and cut it into the shape of their child's state. On a given day, all the cakes came to school, were pieced and iced together, and then were eaten by everyone. The superintendent of the district, community leaders, and the local media attended the official "cutting of the country," giving the event a star-studded scene. Quality education is fun and engaging. Quality education helps students pass state-mandated tests without stress or drill. Students in that particular school easily passed their state-mandated tests, because quality projects enhance learning and improve scores.

Unless districts, administrators, and teachers accept the concept of the school as a living organism, the focus of the school remains the next state report, meaningless meetings, and other bureaucratic trivia. Instead of the school being alive, the bureaucracy flourishes. Trivial forms and meetings become ends in themselves. We serve a dysfunctional system rather than for the children. The organism grows diseases like illiteracy and complacency instead of nurturing children to become responsible adults.

A living school must continue to work on the health of its body. The health of the body becomes better or worse every day. A school doesn't remain static. It needs to grow, or it will fester and die. Just as a healthy body needs nutrition and exercise, a healthy school needs massive doses of humanity, skill, and caring. Those massive doses are the lifeline for the living school. Principals are head doctors for the living school. They provide intravenous feeding in the form of food and drink for the staff on long staff development or teacher conference days. They nourish their staff by defending them. They are heroes for the staff when they model professionalism, enthusiasm, and passion for learning. They exemplify leadership when they attend a difficult seminar at an inconvenient time or place so they can transmit the information to the staff. They never send their staff where they are not willing to go first.

The living school operates within a physical plant, so the quality and maintenance of the facility should be a district priority. Yes, the buildings may be old, and some are decrepit and falling apart. However, we must never accept certain scenarios. First, the teachers, parents, and community must fight at every board meeting for proper maintenance and repairs of school buildings. I have seen and heard of many cases where plumbing, electrical, and carpentry work done in schools was so deficient that if it had been done in my house, I would not pay the contractor and would probably sue for damages. Just like we treat students like our own children, we must treat our schools and classrooms like our second home. Stop accepting incompetence. I think many people would actually be surprised to see quality workmanship when new windows or doors get installed in our schools. We would be amazed if an asbestos cleanup went well and stayed on schedule. Why? Because inner-city schools are draped in the culture of incompetence, and we are conditioned to accept failure.

Teachers and students deserve to work and learn in clean buildings. There may be graffiti on the outer walls and a leaky roof, but we should expect clean and healthy rooms—on a daily basis. I worked with one principal who walked around the school with a can of Comet an hour before the opening bell. He demanded a clean building but was willing to do his part. Teachers and administrators shouldn't accept floors that haven't been swept in a few days or overflowing garbage cans that are not emptied on a regular basis. Floors should be washed, scraped, and waxed during breaks. Desks, bulletin boards, and chalkboards should be cleaned and repaired. Children should be able to use bathrooms that have stall doors that work, toilets that flush, and enough toilet tissue. We should expect the same sanitary conditions at work as they would at home. We shouldn't accept anything less.

While I was teaching at the performing arts school, the board and superintendent decided to privatize the custodial staff. Our outstanding head custodian greeted his new team one afternoon. They were all very nice ladies who didn't speak a word of English. He couldn't tell them how, what, or where to clean.

That same school had a power unit that provided heat or air conditioning. To operate the system, one just had to close and secure the doors. One day I decided to open the doors of the unit very wide to see if there was a filter inside. I don't know if there was a filter, but there sure was a science experiment growing in there. I asked an administrator if there was any scheduled maintenance program. I was assured that people came to inspect the units, and no bad air circulated in the rooms. So we continued to work with runny noses and congested sinuses. The physical discomfort was nothing compared to the debilitating spirits caused by disinterest.

New construction in inner-city school districts can be a comedy of errors. One of the high schools in my district was bulging at the seams in the late sixties and early seventies. Instead of building an additional school, the board of education attached an annex to the original building. The connecting hallways did not mesh into the old to look like one big school. The open area for sports had to be eliminated, so students had to walk several blocks for gym classes. The heating and cooling systems never worked properly in the new patchwork school. Some rooms were very hot, and some very cold.

Who thinks of these things? Better yet, how do they get away with it?

One of the best inner-city schools I ever worked in was burned to the ground. The new facility had a play area on the roof that the children never used because of shoddy workmanship. The building shook for several years because the roof was not attached properly. A national scandal would have erupted if that had happened in a wealthy school district. The building doesn't shake any longer, but the students still do not play on the roof.

Unfortunately, stories like that are all too common in inner-city schools. The culture of incompetence accepts such behavior as the norm. People think, "inner cities are corrupt, so why shouldn't I get my piece of the action?"

If teachers work in dilapidated buildings, they must make every effort to make the building livable. Again, it is a question of school culture. The outside of the building may look like a dungeon, but the inside can contain a vibrant learning community. It is the teacher's responsibility to make the classroom bright, cheery, and an environment conducive to learning.

How can someone maximize the existing situation? He can find free posters at a travel agency to cover peeling plaster or paint. National Geographic distributed four-by-six-foot laminated maps of the world to each classroom in the country one year. That map covered a lot of ugly walls in Paterson that year. He can cover demoralizing spaces with timelines and science projects. I had so many timelines in my high school history classes that my caricature in the yearbook had a timeline on my tie. What can possibly boost children's self-esteem more than to see their work hanging up on a wall? Wow! A child who gets no praise or encouragement in a dysfunctional family has a teacher who actually thinks her work is so good that it should be hung in the hall. Nothing exemplifies the climate of a school like active, engaged children doing projects and proudly showing their work.

Some schools do not have an available classroom for art instruction. Teachers use a wagon or cart and travel from room to room. Art-on-a-cart can be a negative or a positive experience. Again, it depends on where your spirit lies. Have you accepted the culture of incompetence, or are you a member of a living school?

One art teacher in a small school in Paterson was a spectacular member of that living school. Each year, he checked with the social studies teachers in the upper grades for curriculum input. Students then created a mural that complemented their social studies learning. The hallways of that third floor became an extension of the classroom. Not only was it beautiful and bright, but it was also evidence that children were learning—in one of the oldest school buildings in the state.

One of the most memorable moments of my teaching career came when we hatched eggs in the classroom. A fellow teacher had provided us with a small incubator and fertilized eggs. The children actually heard the chicks break through the shells and saw them fight for life. The windows in our classroom were old, and the button latches did not work well, so I wired the windows closed that night, because it was winter, and the baby chicks were still wet. As I entered the room early the next morning, I noticed immediately that the room was frigid. One of the wires had snapped. God sent my very good friend— the district's science supervisor—to my class soon after

I arrived. We grabbed some aquarium tubing and fake fur used for static electricity experiments. We warmed the chicks with the fur and gave them "mouth-to-beak" resuscitation. Much to the children's glee, the chicks survived. Those decaying windows did not kill the chicks or defeat the spirit of my students.

Teachers shouldn't ever accept the terrible conditions that await you in an inner-city classroom. If they accept corruption, incompetence, and complacency, then they have become part of the problem instead of part of the solution.

A living school can function well, even in an old facility, if the head of that organism is an outstanding leader. Principals must be the instructional leaders of the school, and it is their responsibility to create a climate that fosters learning. Positive attitudes and vibrations must begin with the principal. It is the principal's responsibility to combat the culture of incompetence with the culture of learning. Mission statements are ignored sheets of paper in most schools, but quality teachers can recognize the real or de facto mission of the principal within the first month of school. The principal's mission must clear and simple: "Everyone who enters this building is responsible for the education, safety, and growth of children. People will act in a professional manner between and among staff members and as surrogate parents toward children." The principal is the leader, lightning rod, and shoulder for the entire staff. It is a daunting, task.

A staff can be a forest of many different trees. Sometimes a principal needs to address the forest and sometimes the individual trees. Let's look at the trees first. Greet all teachers and staff members as they enter the office every morning—"Hi, how's your daughter? Is she over her flu?" Personal comments of concern build a mutual feeling of trust and humanity that can carry a school staff through rough times. If the goal is to have children come to school eagerly each day, shouldn't it begin with treating teachers personally and professionally so they come to school eagerly? School leaders should walk around the building and comment positively on activities and projects that actively engage students in learning. They should be highly visible but positive forces throughout the school. I have had the privilege of working with and for several outstanding school leaders. They smile in spite of enormous stress and strain. They are human beings who understand that other caring human beings share the goal of quality education for all students.

In addition to treating the staff individually, the principal must look at the teachers as a cohesive team—the forest. The team must develop a chemistry that reflects the personality and professionalism of the principal, who then must have the ability to manage and lead the increasingly diverse group of teachers in schools. The challenge is to meld various styles, cultures, and abilities into a team that loves to work hard for children. Teachers need to trust the leadership of their principal, and the principal must establish a zone of comfort for the staff. In a very real sense, teaching in an inner-city school is like going to battle every day. The teachers face enemies in the streets, the bureaucracy, and the culture of incompetence. They need to feel like the principal is on their side, willing to fight with them and for them. There is a strong parallel between the trust and respect between teacher and student and the trust and respect between principal and teacher.

Instructional leadership must complement personal leadership. Teachers must not only trust the principal as a person but also her ability to create an environment for learning. It is not good enough to simply house children like a jail does. Once the students and teachers are safe in their classes, then what happens? The goal is to educate them not just to keep them safe from harm. The principal must prepare staff development workshops that emphasize learning rather than simply how to enter and exit the cafeteria. Teachers must leave the building every day, thinking, "This is a place where we teach children." If dedicated teachers don't have that feeling in their souls, then the incompetent teacher wins again. That teacher can walk out the door looking like they just walked out of a salon, thinking, "I fooled them again." The living school needs spirit to flow through its veins. Enthusiasm for one's job is almost as important as respect for the children. Children need to see happy and excited teachers and administrators enter the building each day. It's so important that it bears repeating: why should children want to come to school each day when the teachers don't seem to be happy to come to school each day?

School spirit games and activities are vital to the inner-city school. School leaders should let the students and teachers combine ideas to create a colorful physical education uniform. They should empower the students to select certain days of the month for spirit days. They need to bring life to the school. The goal is clear. We want students to see their school as an oasis from the realities of the street—"I like to go to school. It's fun, and we learn there."

Some veterans of the teaching wars may look upon my living school as a corny, quixotic dream. It is not a dream. I have seen real, living schools where teachers hug each other like lifelong friends and treat children like family members. Adults and children look forward to going to school each day. It is not easy, but building a living school can be a stimulating experience. There is a little negative man sitting on everyone's shoulders that will tell you it is impossible. But if teachers refuse to accept the culture of incompetence, they have overcome the first major hurdle. The rest is positive energy, stress, and fun. Our children are worth it.

A school will always have a culture of its own, whether teachers work at it or not. It can be negative, self-defeating, and demoralizing, or it can be beacon of positive vibrations, hope, and excitement. The living school can be the centerpiece of the assault on the culture of incompetence. All stakeholders must work to make their schools living environments for teachers and students to thrive and learn. Choose to live rather than to exist in the status quo of incompetence, racism, and politics.

CLASSROOM INSTRUCTION

If It's Not Tested, It's Not Taught

Many inner-city principals are overwhelmed by security issues inside and outside of the building—violence, guns, and overcrowded classrooms. It takes an incredible leader to remember the true purpose for that large building: the instruction of children. I have found that most principals are concerned for their students, but the tsunami of negative factors can destroy their beachhead of instructional plans. Long-range planning can fall by the wayside as principals try to just get through the day. The difficult job of being a quality principal got exponentially harder with the advent of state testing.

The Standards and Assessment Movement of the last few decades has added tremendous pressure to the already challenging job of the school leader. The overt or covert message from the central office is always "raise the test scores." Bureaucrats at the local, national, and federal level often confuse instruction with assessment and standards with assessment. Instruction is teaching; assessment is the measurement of that teaching. Standards are the bar, and assessment is the measurement of success in reaching that bar. Prepping students for a state test for a significant period of time is not in the child's best interest. It is in the interests of superintendents, state education officials, and local real estate agents who want to read a headline in the newspaper that scores rose in the city. The tragedy lies in the fact that all our eggs are in one basket. Our children's future rests on tests whose validity is often challenged. Instead of mandating a curriculum that includes quality works of literature in language arts classes, district officials purchase consumable books with such titles as *Strategies and Techniques* in order to pass a state test. The assessment bureaucrats working at the state level distribute practice test questions to prepare students for the test. Some districts then hire private companies to produce more practice questions so we can drill the students to death. Maybe scores will rise a few percentages because students have practiced similar questions. But what have they learned?

I totally understand and agree with the idea of taking time on a regular basis to review concepts for a state test and even to develop test-taking skills. However, if a school or district must spend months prepping for a test, then their original instructional plan was either flawed or nonexistent.

My boss at one time was the director of curriculum. When she left, her position was not filled for over a year. The importance of curriculum at that time for that district was clear: "If it is not tested, don't teach it, and don't fund it." The state appointed a superintendent, and the district sold its soul to the pressures of state bureaucrats. They stopped teaching children and prepped them, like trained seals, to pass a questionable test. Leaders only thought of making themselves look good instead of putting the children first.

A primordial, significant question must be asked. Why can't children in inner-city schools pass the state tests at the same rate as schools in wealthier, suburban areas? In all my years as teacher, administrator, district supervisor, and state committee member, I've never heard that question asked. All stakeholders should have asked themselves that question, and then inner-city schools could have faced the issues confronting city children together. Was the question never asked because the stakeholders felt they knew the answer? Did ignorance and bigotry stop them from an intelligent discussion of the question?

I have always believed that all children can learn as long as the playing field is made fair and level. All races and ethnicities can learn equally, if all members of society work hard to ensure equity. However, if we assume that poor children can't learn anyway, then it is easy to accept the drill-and-kill test prep mentality. We need to have faith in our children and believe that they can learn and succeed if given world-class curriculum guides, excellent teachers, and diverse, engaging instruction. We need to believe that parental responsibility, reduction of poverty, and students working hard are the path to success. If we accept the culture of incompetence as the norm, then we perpetuate the existence of illiteracy, crime, and overcrowded jails.

The focus of any important, state testing meeting must be the refusal to accept the culture of incompetence as the norm. Such meetings should demand the social, political, and economic changes necessary to give all children a fair chance at passing the tests. When all children are given the opportunity of quality instruction, then we can compare districts. Until that time comes, all we do is cover up the real problems with wasteful preparations for unreliable tests. I am absolutely convinced that, when all stakeholders work together to provide equality of opportunity in all schools, all students can easily pass any state-mandated tests.

All inner-city boards of education must take a stand and create challenging curriculum guides that become the marching orders for quality instruction. Quality instruction is impossible without a stimulating, thorough curriculum. Classroom management is impossible without quality instruction. All the best practices in education are related. The strategies for success are as interwoven as the negative factors that destroy schools.

Students in an inner-city school district need an intense, thorough curriculum equal to the best suburban schools. If we accept the concept that inner-city children come to school in kindergarten further behind their counterparts in suburbia because of poverty and other socioeconomic conditions, then why aren't we trying to catch up instead of dumbing lessons down? Shouldn't the school be the vehicle to drive students to overcome the debilitating effects of life in the inner city?

Let's find the best schools in our state, and create a curriculum that equals them in quality and excellence. I want one superintendent in an inner-city school district to have the guts to call the most successful school district in the state to borrow its curriculum guides. I want that superintendent to slam those guides down on a table during the next district meeting and ask, "Why doesn't ours look like this?" I never witnessed anyone in the higher echelons of power in the Paterson School District contact the Mountain Lakes or Milburns of the state to compare curricula guides. I did see a carousel of people in authority move from Newark to Paterson to Jersey City, padding their resumes with new titles. All three districts were operated by the state at one time because of gross incompetence, yet each district hired each others' brain trust.

Curriculum committees must include the best teachers, administrators, and community members possible. Too often, the same people reply to postings for curriculum committees because they think it is an easy way to make some extra money. Leaders should make it a competitive process where people earn places on the committee because of their abilities, experience, and vision.

That committee must then create a guide so thorough that it looks like a teacher resource guide. A new teacher should be able to pick up the guide and feel assured that he knows what content must be taught for the entire year and what the best practices are to implement that content. A national expert on curriculum should be able to pick up the district guide and believe that, if implemented properly, a child will master national standards. Do we owe our children anything less? Wouldn't if be wonderful if a child graduating from high school in an inner-city school looked at national standards during one of his college classes and said, "Yeah, I learned that."

Curriculum guides must be the bibles for all teachers, especially new ones. It provides their marching orders as they try to touch the lives of many children. It is almost a history of best practices that have succeeded in the past. No army can succeed without a great battle plan. The curriculum guide is the educational plan. Caring teachers who have developed a warm rapport with their students can implement the plan and know that children will learn. Children who are learning have no time to misbehave. The brains behind classroom management must be a thorough, creative, engaging curriculum.

The only way schools will succeed is if children succeed. Children succeed when they are taught well, challenged with a quality curriculum, and pushed by caring, competent teachers. Instruction is the key. All stakeholders in the educational process have the responsibility to create the cocoon for teachers and students to thrive.

Curriculum guides throughout the country are very similar. Is United States history different in Kansas, Texas, or New York? Are physics or chemistry different subjects in different states? Why are children in affluent communities taught a more challenging, comprehensive version of subjects? Isn't it the grossest form of racism to dumb down a curriculum for inner-city children? Do we allow our preconceived racial perceptions to form our level of expectations?

The quality of instruction in inner-city classrooms can be as diverse as the student body itself. It ranges from creative and brilliant to incompetent and destructive. Many inner-city teachers create quality plans and interesting activities in spite of the people who are supposed to help them—not because of them.

I have personally witnessed excellence that brought tears to my eyes, because I knew what the teacher had to do to successfully implement her plan. I have seen mock trials from grades two to twelve, community redevelopment plans created by students in all grades, and of course, the amazing high school students who won the state National History Day contest almost every year. All those teachers should be the heroes of the district; they should be praised and supported by all stakeholders. They should not feel isolated or as though they are struggling against a tide of incompetence. They should be riding on the wave of change.

The quality of instruction can be abysmal in many inner-city classrooms. Old textbook and ditto activities are followed by textbook and ditto activities. Children are bored and fail. The more they fail, the more textbook and ditto activities they get—at a lower level. Incompetence is a self-perpetuating phenomenon. The more the students fail, the less and less is taught and learned. It is a vicious spiral. Poor teaching is followed by poor teaching, as teachers blame everyone but themselves for the failure of students to learn. Teachers give close-minded lessons assessed by open book tests. If a student is quiet, his lowest grade is a C. If some incompetent teachers had to sit through their own lessons, they would jump out of the first window they could open.

Great instruction begins with excellent teachers preparing interesting, diverse, and challenging lessons. Students in excellent schools have a rich, stable structure at home for support. They have a stake in the system, and they know that learning and passing are key to future success. Whether they think school is a game or not, they are players, because they know it is important and that they can succeed if they pass. Many students in quality schools can survive a mediocre or poor teacher because they have support at home or in the community.

Inner-city students need years of quality teachers in a row. They need quality teachers who inspire, challenge, and believe in them. Inner-city students need to be convinced that they can succeed. They don't believe in themselves or in the system. Put a textbook on their desks and a teacher in front of them who lectures or reads it aloud all day, and they tune out immediately. "I am a failure in school, and I have a failure as a teacher." As I have often repeated, failure breeds failure, and the spiral is always downward. So the failures get greater and more severe each year. That failure can lead to a life in jail, or multiple unwanted pregnancies for females.

"Student-centered learning" and "active learners" are terms we hear often in education. They are strategies that are essential in the inner-city school. Students must be engaged and active learners. They must be convinced that learning is important and that they have a chance to be successful in school and the community.

One of the most tragic fallacies in urban education is that less planning is necessary because the students learn less or more slowly than students in effective schools. Students in failing schools need the highest quality lesson plans just like they need the highest quality teachers. The further behind the student is academically, the more thoughtful and interesting the lesson plans need to be. Usually a "slow" group of students in an ineffective school gets basic, boring, drill-and-kill types of lessons. The materials are much lower than the grade level, but sometimes the tease is that the materials are "high interest." If students successfully complete a text that is several years behind their grade level, what have they accomplished? They are seventh graders who received an A on a fifth-grade test.

What type of lesson plan is most effective in failing schools? Lesson plans must engage the students in the learning process. The lessons must empower the students to assume responsibility for their learning. Students must be active learners in the process. Instruction must include learning that begins with the student's experiences in life but expands their knowledge to places they have never seen. Teachers can't limit instruction to the students' experiences. That is a great place to start, but teaching Hispanic, Korean, or African-American students only their own culture and history confines them to what they already know. They must experience the language, history, and science of the mainstream culture so they can develop dreams and goals of success.

"Engage" and "empower" are two chic verbs in education. People with titles often need to invent new terms to justify their jobs. However, those two verbs are very much on target in the instructional process. Think about what an inner-city child owns or has the authority to control. He has very little ownership over material things and very little control over other issues in his life. If he can claim ownership over a school project, do you think he will remember the experience longer than the practice worksheet to a test? I remember an ethnic festival that the students and teachers planned and carried out together like it was yesterday—I was in seventh grade.

There was a nonprofit foundation in the city of Paterson that provided teachers and students with grants for innovative projects. My eighth grade class decided to build an environmental center on our school grounds. We won the grant and created the plans. A local concrete company donated cement and poured our slab for nothing—everyone is a stakeholder. My students carried lumber, sawing wood, and nailing the building together. They were boys and girls from a housing project that had a horrible record of drugs and crime, and they were working together in harmony. For years after the project was completed, there was never any graffiti on our center, yet there was plenty of graffiti on the school building. Why? It was their center.

I once found a design to build all the planets to scale in size and distance from the sun, that would work perfectly for my eighth grade class, which was at the intersection of two long corridors. The children loved the idea and quickly made each planet out of balloons and papier mâché. We painted the planets and accurately hung them along the longer of the two corridors. The children were very proud of their project. A student from another class knocked the earth down and stuffed it into the boys' commode. At the end of the day, one of my students ran into class, frantically yelling, "Mr. C, the earth is going down the toilet!" Looking around at my old classroom that needed new desks and a paint job, I said, "I know." It was a magical moment, but I was struck by how sincere and upset the student was. It was his solar system.

Can we think of other school assignments that would get students so upset? I have seen countless other quality projects that are much better than the ones I have described. They all have the same aspects in common. Students are given responsibility and authority over their work. The assignments are fun and meaningful. Everyone remembers them for a long time.

Students in ineffective schools in the inner cities have experienced a lifetime of failure, lies, and false hope. They have been told over and over again that they don't count and that they are just biding their time in school. As I have said, some schools are simply holding cells for the county jail. The teacher chalks and talks, hands out dittos—mainly for control and discipline—and the day ends slowly with little or no instruction. Children recognize a teacher who wants to include them in the instructional process; they will be a friend and learner for life—"Mrs. Smith thinks enough of me to make me take responsibility for my learning and includes me in planning how the lesson is taught. Wow." The affective result to an instructional activity will be as great as or greater than the cognitive knowledge and skills learned. The residual effect will be a student who looks forward to coming to class, saying, "I need to do well because Mrs. Smith thinks I'm important." The student learns pride in her work and success. She thinks, "I can do this!"

I worked part time for the New Jersey Center for Civic and Law-Related Education. That center encourages teachers to utilize dynamic activities that engage students in the process of learning civics. One of my favorite activities is called a continuum. It is really a spectrum of opinions. The teacher presents a controversial issue or an interesting question with a yes or no answer that relates to the students' life experiences. "Should a curfew for teenagers be established in a town due to the increased level of crime and drug activity late at night?" was one of my favorite continuum questions. Students who support the question wholeheartedly stand on one side of the continuum line, and students who oppose it strongly stand on the other end. Students judge where on the line they should stand. This is a kinesthetic, thinking activity that forces students to listen and evaluate their friends' opinions. Students love it and remember it for weeks.

When I taught high school social studies, students knew that we would form a circle to discuss a controversial issue, several times a month. I always chose a topic related to the curriculum, looking for one that might affect their lives personally. They needed to think and discuss fairly, and respect their classmates' opinions. The discussion was always followed by a writing assignment. It sure did beat a boring worksheet.

Boring busywork centered on worksheet after worksheet only encourages discipline problems. All children of the twenty-first century have been raised in a culture of instant gratification and the entertain-me-now mind-set. Computers and video games over stimulate children with fantastic imagery and nonstop action. Inner-city children are surrounded by more stimuli with loud, violent, crowded streets and sometimes broken, dysfunctional families. Boring, watered down curricula dull the senses and can be very frustrating. When frustration reaches a boiling point, major discipline problems occur. We create our own monsters with a dull curriculum, which leads to ineffective instruction. If qualified, sensitive teachers are the soul of classroom management, then a great curriculum guide implemented by those great teachers is certainly the brains behind effective classroom management.

I have observed many classrooms in my career, and I have noticed a disturbing trend in classroom instruction. Too many teachers pander to their children instead of educating them—"We are having a quiz tomorrow, but don't worry. I didn't make it too hard. In fact, here are the two essay questions that you should study tonight. Tomorrow, you will have twenty minutes to study before you take the quiz. If you are having trouble, you can open your textbooks for the last few minutes of the test to check your answers." If I were a student in that class, I would never study. Why should I?

Life can be tough. Work can be hard. Start studying.

In addition to pandering to students, we have substituted quantity for quality in the work we accept from students. Some say, "I did all the worksheets you gave us. Why didn't I get an A on my report card?" Class worksheets carry the same weight on a report card as tests. How can that be possible? The quality of a student's work must be valued higher than the quantity of worksheets he submits. Will their bosses give him worksheets when he is an adult, or will he be expected to think, solve problems, and create? Let us choose quality as our yardstick for success.

Parents play a major role in reviewing their children's schoolwork. If someone's children receive an A on a report card without seeing substantial work, then something is wrong. Your children should not receive an A just because they are well behaved and complete their schoolwork. They should earn an A because they have mastered the material and have demonstrated that mastery in projects or tests. If parents are only interested in their children getting A's so they can get into a good college, then that mentality will only damage their child in the future. Sooner or later—in college or a career position—they will need to demonstrate their abilities, which does not mean completing ditto number fifteen. Parents are stakeholders, and they have a choice. Parents need to fight for quality of instruction.

If we are to improve instruction in inner-city schools, then we must accept certain prerequisites. Poverty and racism have combined to destroy many families in inner-city neighborhoods. Those broken families are faced with the challenges of guns, violence, drugs, and abuse. If we accept those facts as unfortunate truths, then we must admit that those families may be less stable, structured, and disciplined.

Children from those families spend most of their days at an institution we call school. That school must be more stable, structured, and disciplined than the home. Stability, structure, and discipline mean functionally strong schools with quality curriculum and instruction. Students need to look at the clock and say, "Wow, where did the day go?"

MESSAGES TO THE STAKEHOLDERS

Choices

A beautiful, intelligent Hispanic young woman prepares to go to school on a very cold morning. She is a member of a warm, loving family that came to America to pursue the dream that millions before them have chased. Her doting father goes into the garage to warm the car before taking his children to school. Moments later, she enters the garage to find that her father has been fatally wounded by criminals trying to steal the family car.

The many problems facing inner-city schools are as interwoven as a spider's web. No one problem can be fixed without addressing them all simultaneously. Therefore, all stakeholders in the process of educating children must do their appropriate parts to solve the problems. Those stakeholders include federal and state officials, all educators, parents, students, the media, and community members. No group can escape part of the blame, and all groups must work together to solve the mess. No one can point fingers unless they point at the mirror. All stakeholders have choices to make concerning the education of our next generation of American citizens. These are complex choices when one discusses the problems of inner-city education.

The essence of a democracy is opportunity. All citizens, regardless of socioeconomics, race, or ethnicity must have the opportunity to achieve the American Dream with hard work and determination. That is one of the cornerstone beliefs of our country. Thomas Jefferson told us that the pursuit of happiness is an inalienable right bestowed by our Creator. It is the mandate of all stakeholders to ensure that the playing field where youngsters struggle to reach the American Dream is level and fair. There is the profound belief that all men are created equal under God and implicit with that belief is the concept of equality of opportunity. What people do with that opportunity is their choice. All stakeholders must work together to make sure that all children have a fair and equal choice.

The battle for the American Dream can be found in the daily struggles of individuals and families who strive to make a living so that their children can have a better life than them. It is the game of American life. All of us must believe that we are viable members of the game with a legitimate chance at success if we work hard and obey the rules. American children from functioning families who attend effective schools know the rules and work hard to succeed in order to please themselves and their parents.

As I have previously stated, there are children in middle and high school in the inner city who know that they are not in the lineup of life. They are not a member of the team striving for the American Dream. If a child in the inner city doesn't feel like he is part of the system growing up, he will become an apathetic adult, a career criminal, or a dysfunctional ward of the state. It is the responsibility of all the stakeholders to put every child on a team that is fighting for the American Dream. Schools, communities, politicians, parents, and the media must do their parts, and likewise the students must respond with responsible behavior of their own. People who choose not to join the struggle for the American Dream have no one to blame but themselves. Opportunity is implicit in the birth of every American, and both the powerful and the neglected have choices to make when opportunity knocks.

More importantly, if all citizens don't believe in the opportunity to succeed, then the democracy is in danger. If the public school system fails to prepare young adults for that challenge, then we will have a country of the few rich, a struggling middle class, and the permanently poor. The gap between rich and poor is widening in this country and that is partly a result of our failing public school system. Some children in inner-city schools can barely read by twelfth grade, and they have very few skills in a competitive, information-age world. They have no stake in the system. They get passed from one grade level to the next without the skills necessary for success. Whatever fancy term we give to the pass-them-along system, it is still social promotion. Social promotion moves students through and out of the system and keeps the retention statistics on the school report cards palatable.

Some wealthy and some middle-class students know they must succeed in school so they can go to college and get a good job. It's what their parents want, and it is the way to live well. If I am thirteen years old in the seventh grade in an inner-city school and can't read or write, what are my chances of success? I am not in the game of life. I'm a spectator in the cheap seats. Why should I stay? Why should I behave? There were days when I would sadly watch my classes work silently. Are there students sitting in front of me who are already doomed to a life of dependency and failure? Who has the best chance to survive in the real, adult world?

It is long past due for our stakeholders to make some choices. It is time our country made the education of all children its top priority. Nothing short of national security should bump educating children from the top of our priorities. The compass of our country must always point to *C* for child. If the country doesn't want to take the time or reserve the resources to prepare the next generation of leaders, then what kind of country will we have in the near future?

I believe our country has lost its moral purpose. We have become slaves to materialism and sensationalism. Drug- or alcohol-addicted celebrities are our teenagers' heroes. We need documentary reports on television that tell parents that it is good for them to prepare a family meal that is attended by all members. Our children demand the latest in fashion, and we buy it regardless of appropriateness of the outfit for the age of the child. As the Paterson principal who became famous for his bat and bullhorn said, "If you have Calvin Klein on your behind, you have nothing on your mind." (I disagreed with everything else he said.)

Several years ago, I saw a picture of the Washington Monument with scaffolding surrounding all its sides. If our inner-city children are to succeed, they must be like that monument—strong and with a solid foundation of scaffolding stakeholders to support them. If our society truly wants inner-city children to succeed, then it must be the scaffold and grow with the child as she struggles through life. It is our responsibility and duty. Students must respond to the stakeholders and utilize the resources provided by the scaffold to be successful. It is their responsibility and duty. Everyone must make choices.

No one should expect inner-city students to be superheroes in order to succeed in life. That is totally unfair. Students must however, recognize that education is the vehicle to escape the horrors of poverty, drugs, and crime. They must also recognize the dangers of the streets and the lure of quick money or superficial happiness. All stakeholders must support students as they try to recognize both facts, but the students themselves must bear their share of the responsibility. If there are community, religious, or governmental programs to support students, they should go for it. They shouldn't wait for the programs or blame the lack of those programs for their decisions to not work hard in school, stay out all night, or participate in activities and scenarios that are dangerous to your health and chances at success. It takes more than one person or entity to form a relationship. Students must respond to the network of people and groups who are helping build their support scaffold. When the network provides students with the advice and materials for success, they must not throw them away.

Students in successful schools pay attention in class and participate in lessons, activities, and programs. They do that because they want to be in the game of life and they want future financial and personal success. They don't do it because they are white. For students to choose not to take notes, pass tests, or do homework because they might "act white" is absurd and self-destructive. Some people will deliberately keep children out of the game of life for selfish or racist motives, but for them to choose not to enter the game gives those racist actions validity—"See. Even they don't care about themselves."

It doesn't take a grown white man like me to tell any minority student that life will difficult for them. Socioeconomics and racism hinder many minority children from birth. That child always seems to play catch-up throughout his or her life. As the census figures illustrate very clearly, in this country, poverty is centered on single women and children. If a young, inner-city teenage male engages in casual, unprotected sex, then his actions are irresponsible and criminal. You are committing a crime against society, your female partner, and your ethnic group when you impregnate a woman and then walk away from your responsibility. Yes, it is much worse for an inner-city male to perform that deed than for a middle- or upper-class male who commits the same act of irresponsibility. Your actions have deliberately put the child further behind at the start of life and actually helped to keep that child out of the game of life. It is immorality at its lowest point. The immorality has nothing to do with the morals of having sex at an early age. That is a private choice for you. However, when you know how difficult it is to succeed in the inner city and carelessly place your child even further behind where you started, that is even more egregious. Shame on you and the choice you made.

Our country is a country of immigration. The origin and language of the immigrants have changed throughout history, but they all come to America looking for a better life. My grandfather came to America from Italy at age thirteen. He barely had enough money for a cheap ticket on the ship of dreams. His voyage was so bad, he never returned to visit his native country. He began working soon after entering the country and knew that he had to learn some English in order to work in the country. How else could he communicate with his bosses?

Immigrants today have the luxury of quicker travel to and from their native country due to the invention of the airplane. They can also purchase phone cards to call family that was left behind. Unfortunately, that leads many new immigrants to speak of their native country as "my country." Immigrant children who attend American schools and whose families plan to live and work in this country must consider the United States their country. How else can students succeed educationally, socially, and economically if they do not even consider the place they live to be their country? They need to choose America and become American so they and the schools in the inner city have a chance for success.

The streets are the enemy of any inner-city family trying to succeed in life. There are many stories of families who have been hardworking citizens and still lost a child to the street. I never encountered a better family than the one mentioned in the opening narrative of this chapter, and yet they lost their father. The streets are predatory and relentless.

All stakeholders must assist young children to choose work, family, and school over the lure of the streets. Again, young people need to assume some of the responsibility. They need to learn the difference between right and wrong at an early age from a parent, grandparent, guardian, or any role model. Some young people in the inner city do not have one or two parents but do have a responsible adult to teach them right from wrong. That is why the stakeholders must be as relentless as the streets in fighting for and with young people. As I have said many times, the problems of inner-city schools are complex and interwoven like a spider's web. All problems must be addressed simultaneously by all stakeholders if we have any chance of success.

Additionally, health problems plague many young people living in the inner city. Environmental factors such as dilapidated housing can cause diseases, such as asthma. Poor eating habits can lead to hypertension and obesity. Alcohol, drugs, and guns can be found as easily as a candy bar. Those factors are all part of the stranglehold of the streets. Students can't assist the streets in their own destruction. They need to clean their rooms and their clothes. They need to learn about proper diet, even if it means cooking for themselves. They need to participate in gym classes and other exercise programs found in places like a Boys and Girls Club or a YMCA. They need to be proactive against the streets and not be willing volunteers. There is a fine line between being a victim and a volunteer. Students shouldn't point a finger at other stakeholders for their problems, if they have not done their share.

It is totally un-American for any young person to be kept out of the game of life. No young person should willingly drop out of the game for the short-term enjoyment of the streets. If he wants to be successful, he must be in the mainstream game of life. Where are the successful jobs, the good schools, and the safe streets? Where does he want to live? He needs to dress and talk like he wants to be successful. Why have young people modeled themselves after criminals by wearing their pants below their butts? Why would a business owner want to hire a young person after he has seen his underwear? The child needs to comb his hair, take the rag off, and hold his hat when he enters a building.

There is one English language. Rules for grammar are found in English textbooks in all high schools in America. There aren't different rules in New York, Chicago, or Los Angeles. If children expect to work in a successful, mainstream business, they need to speak mainstream American English, not some illiterate nonsense some people pass off as a cultural language. We must promote success, and success means speaking in an educated manner.

Students do not need to give up any of their cultural enjoyments because they speak English correctly, dress appropriately, and comb their hair. No one is asking them to give up their roots or heritage. One of the definitions of success is the ability to function in the majority, mainstream culture. Dressing and talking "ghetto" defines a student as a ghetto resident for life. Why limit himself to the environment that may be destroying him? He needs to expand his horizons and join the game of life. Students have difficult choices to make in life. There are people willing to support their struggles, but they have to bear their share of the work and responsibility. Students need to choose life, not instant gratification.

What do good parents do for their children? A father is not someone who simply makes babies. That is the easy part. There is a major difference between a male who makes babies and a dad. Most women, likewise, can reproduce. Not all women who reproduce are mothers. Adults who choose to become parents must know and understand the lifetime responsibilities of parenthood. A student who chooses to become a parent is a fool.

Real parents read to their children from birth, set parameters for their children's behavior, and fight for them and with them on all important issues. Real parents know where their children are at all times of the day. They watch what their children eat, what they watch on television, and what video games they play.

I will repeat that all stakeholders must help and be parents, if necessary, in their fight for children. The phrase "It takes a village" is never more meaningful than in the inner city. Parents in or on the cusp of poverty may have to work two jobs or work second or third shifts at a factory. Who watches their children? We all must watch their children. That means school, church, and community programs. It means the neighbor next door, or an aunt or uncle.

My parents were raised during the Great Depression and had many siblings. Yet if they misbehaved, a neighbor was sure to either cuff them or tell their parents. Police walking the beat knew all the children in the neighborhood and recognized when a child was near danger or in danger.

The streets have so terrorized people in poverty that they live in isolation and fear their neighbors. We need to regain and reform our neighborhoods so neighbors can act like extended family members. Neighbors and friends do not have a choice. They must be that surrogate parent when a child needs one. The spiritual and economic growth of our country depends on the success of our inner cities. We can not continue to have pockets of poverty that feed upon themselves generation after generation. The loss of talent and the draining of funds will destroy our country. We are all in the same national boat. Every American must be a parent to a child who needs one. We can not continue to sit on our porches and watch children go astray. Community police and the clergy must emphasize this point to all citizens.

It is a dangerous, scary world for all children to live in today. When I was ten, I could go to a park, play all day, and just make sure I was home before the streetlights went on. Today, parents can send their children out for the day and never see them again. Some parents are trapped in their own worlds and do not know what is going on in their children's lives. Other parents become helicopter parents, hovering over their children at all times and swooping down at the first sign of trouble. Helicopter parents have great motives, but may inadvertently hurt their children in the end. All children must be taught self-reliance. That is essential for future success. Parents need to make sure their children can solve appropriate problems at a young age. They need projects or chores to build their sense of responsibility. Parents should give them situations in which they must learn self-reliance. Children must assume some of the responsibility for their success in school, but that ability to be responsible doesn't grow overnight. Parents need to raise their children to be winners who know how to walk, talk, and dress like winners.

Everyone must fight for our children and fight with them when necessary. I once had a high school student who drove me nuts over assignments and grades. I would not give up on him, but he sure pushed me to the limit. We never really had many friendly conversations, because I was always in his face when necessary and he was always complaining or making excuses. At the end of the year, we all signed each others' yearbooks. The comment he left on his picture for me was very simple: "Don't change." That comment hit me like a bolt of lightning.

We are all parents to any children who need one.

As a grandparent, it is very easy for me to give into every one of my grandchildren's requests. I do not have the same responsibility as their parents. Parents must say no to some of their children's requests. They must fight for their children and fight with their children at certain times. Parents are the adults.

It is not right for children to be in the streets late at night, especially on a school night. I have driven home from board of education or PTA meetings and watched ten year olds in the streets after ten o'clock at night. That makes no sense.

It is harder for parents in the inner city to be good parents because the dangers are greater. Their children will complain and scream, but they will love their parents more because they stood up to them and the streets.

I worked for a state-appointed superintendent of schools who decried the fact that inner-city children did not have computers at home and had to do their homework at the kitchen table. Where did he think I did my homework as a child? Is there any better visual than a parent sitting with a child at the table doing homework? Isn't that the time for conversations about the day?

Parents must talk to and with their children. "Our neighbor told me he saw you with that boy who always gets into trouble. Why are you playing with him? What did you do after school?" Remember, it is a parent's responsibility to know where her children are at all times. If she does not have the time, ability, or desire to be a great parent, then why be a parent at all? If she is so young that she does not even know who she is, then how can she be that great parent?

Parents are the primary stakeholders in the education of their children. Their choices are first and paramount in their children's lives. Their support is the first floor of the scaffold. There is no manual that guarantees success as a parent. However, all adults who conceive children must make the choice to work hard to raise those children to the best of their abilities and to fight the forces that will tear down the support scaffold around a child's life. People who conceive children with no thought at all have already made their choices.

Parents need to make the right choice. They need to be a fighting role model for their children. They need to be great parents.

Are all forms of media out of control and only interested in money, ratings and sales? Have sensationalism and greed overtaken truth and integrity as motivation for the media? The quick story to beat the competitors gets the front page rather than the truthful, insightful story. The merit of the story is secondary to its immediate impact.

The common good is a term that has been abandoned in the race for ratings.

The common good is an essential theme for a democracy. We give up some of our personal freedoms to join a society that works for the good of all. I am a stout believer in the first amendment to our Bill of Rights, but selfish people must not use that amendment to advance their own greed or interest. All media have a responsibility to the common good. Does the story have merit, or does it just have shock value?

Media moguls are stakeholders in the education of children in the inner city, and they have many choices to make for the common good. Do they want to see a new generation of qualified, informed citizens purchasing their products, or do they want to make the quick buck regardless of ethics? We are asking children in the inner city not to be influenced by the lure of easy, quick money from drugs and violence. Should we not expect the same of the multimillionaires who run our media?

Everyone needs to make choices to break the culture of incompetence in our schools. All stakeholders must attack that culture at the same time and with the same vigor. If teachers try to improve quality instruction but do not get support from the media, businesses, and parents, then the scaffold of support crumbles.

Television and video games can be babysitters for inner-city children before and after school. Adults believe that, as long as the children are off the streets, they are safe. What are the children watching and playing? They are watching shows and commercials that glorify the drug and alcohol lifestyles of the heroes of pop culture. They watch "reality" shows that create heroes out of the most dysfunctional celebrities. Reality must show hardworking, caring parents who strive to provide their children with better lives. Reality must be children working hard in school, believing in the system, and willing to forego easy money. Yet there are many so-called reality shows where self-destructive behavior is championed. No child should watch that nonsense, especially not children who may not have adult role models. Should the latest celebrity who ditches rehab be their hero?

Sports heroes have a major responsibility in our society. Whether they like it or not, they are role models for children who fantasize their future lives to be the lives of sports heroes. The number one sport for children in the inner city is basketball. How can we expect young adults to dress, talk, and walk like successful people in mainstream society, when they watch professional basketball players dress and talk like members of the ghetto culture? Can children in the inner city interview for a job dressed like a "gangsta"? Can we please stop the after game press conferences with rags on our heads and our hats on sideways? Where in the business world do you see people dressed like that? Are we deliberately cultivating and glorifying a culture that can be harmful to young adults in the inner city just to make money? One in a million young boys will ever play professional sports. Yet how many young boys will talk, dress, and act like their sports heroes?

Million-dollar athletes have a responsibility and a choice. If they influence young children to look and act "ghetto," then they condemn those children to a life in the ghetto. Only one in a million will get out to play professional basketball. What will happen to the rest?

We must encourage young adults to dress properly and not to wear their pants so low that their underwear is visible for everyone to see. I walked into a clothing store during a recent Christmas holiday season, and there was a mannequin with its pants deliberately low enough for the mannequin's crack to be showing. Crack kills in more ways than one. How irresponsible was that company for that type of marketing? What choices have they made for the good of the country?

Business owners complain about the young people who apply for a job with little or no skills. They also complain about the number of young people who drop out of school, loiter around, and shoplift in their stores. Those owners have a responsibility to not pander to the latest fad just to make a quick buck. If they want responsible citizens who can work and shop in their stores, then they must be active stakeholders who support the efforts of people who want to break the culture of incompetence in our schools. No person or group can be left on the sidelines if we are to break the cycle of poverty and despair.

In the past, I have called newspapers to cover an event that illustrated hardworking, young adults doing positive things for their communities. I called, but reporters rarely showed up. For many years, one high school in Paterson regularly won the state National History Day competition. Because of one victory, they traveled to Washington DC for the national competition. While I sat with thousands of other high school students at the awards ceremony, I was struck by the lack of diversity in the crowd. Our inner-city students went to bat against the best schools in the country. Do you think that would make a good story?

I introduced the Academic Decathlon to the Paterson district. Again, this was a competition where young inner-city students matched their abilities to read, research, and think about a common topic against the best schools in the state. Don't you think the common good would be served with a lengthy story about their struggles to study, and earn money for the competition?

Media and businesses shouldn't complain about the quality of young adult that leaves an inner-city school if they shirk their responsibilities as stakeholders in the process. They are willing volunteers in the culture of incompetence rather than a positive member of society, trying to destroy it.

Let that same newspaper get a call about guns in schools, and they will send a team of reporters and cameramen. Are they choosing what news stories are good for the community, or are they sensationalizing and creating the news to sell newspapers? Who makes choices like that? Do they really care if children succeed in school and in life? They have a choice to de-emphasize cheap, quick stories that just sell more newspapers. Again, I say that if we are asking our young people in the inner cities not to seek the cheap thrill, we should expect the same from our media moguls.

Newspapers need to follow a positive story that illustrates productive young citizens. The children need the boost, the community needs to know, and it is the newspapers' responsibility as stakeholders to build the scaffold for students to climb out of the poverty of the inner city. We don't need a simple picture with one minority student holding a plaque. We are talking about quality journalism that tells a meaningful story for the betterment of the common good. Remember those types of stories? Let's have stories that glorify the struggles children overcame in order to succeed. Let's have stories in which young adults relish the joy of hard work.

The media has a choice and a responsibility. If it does not want to provide positive stories about quality individuals, then it has chosen to abandon children and create a new generation of young adults who will commit crimes. Then it can perpetuate the stories it really wants to talk about. Shame on the media.

African-Americans have been the one minority group that has suffered the most poverty and discrimination in history. That is no secret or historic discovery. Their history is a story of the middle passage, of slavery, of Jim Crow, and of migrations to Northern cities. Poverty translates into life in the inner city, poor health, and inferior schools.

There have been some major strides in the struggle for economic, political, and social equality. There is a significant black middle class, and it has the opportunity to reach out and pull some family and friends out of the cycle of poverty. That cycle breeds some of the negative factors that have crushed our schools. Breaking the cycle of poverty is one of the main strategies to destroy the culture of incompetence in our poor schools.

African-American students, parents, and business leaders can read about the choices that have already been discussed in previous pages. They must also recognize the uniqueness of their people's historic dilemma and make important choices. There is still systemic racism in this country, but there is a larger group of people who want to see African-American children succeed. They want all children, regardless of color or ethnicity, to have equality of opportunity in housing, jobs, and schools. One hundred percent of all our energy should focus on providing the new generation of young African-American children with a quality education.

There are only a certain number of hours in the day; there is only a certain amount of energy in our lives. African-Americans can use that time and energy to work together with other concerned groups toward the same goal, or they can use their time hating white people for what happened in the past. The culture of incompetence in our schools will not be destroyed if they spend their precious time hating everything white. It is their choice.

I volunteered to be a member of a community group to work on strategies to improve education. It was after school, and as a volunteer, I was not financially compensated. That fact never bothered me, because many teachers donate their time on after-school committees. I attended the first meeting, and a fellow member—an African-American female—challenged me, saying that I could not possibly understand the problems of the community because I lived in a white suburb. Her anger and resentment were palpable. She made a choice to use her time and energy for that tirade instead of working positively for change. I will never feel or understand the pain that person may have encountered during her life in the city. It would have been be presumptuous for me to say, "I understand." However, her body and soul were facing backward not forward.

I also tried to help an excellent, white female teacher who was being accosted by an African-American parent, again claiming that she could not teach her child well because she lived in a white suburb.

Is it time in our history for all Americans to eliminate the word "race" from our national consciousness? Race is a physical description that is rather obsolete. If we discard race, will racism as a term be next for the trash? Children who need quality education are human beings first, and deserve great teachers just because they are human. We sometimes forget that teaching is about one wiser human being influencing the life of an equal, though younger, human being.

Aren't the words "culture" and "ethnicity" more accurate and positive ways to celebrate our differences and similarities? We will soon find out that we are more alike than we are different. How many times do we walk into an upscale restaurant to find a "new" item on the menu that momma made for us many years ago because families were large and money was short? Whether it is pasta *e fagiole* for Italians, chitterlings for African-Americans, or *arroz* and beans for Hispanics, all groups have shared and still share the same miseries and glories of history. Parents—all families fight the same fight. They should join together with other people who want their child to succeed. Great teachers have no particular skin color, religion, ethnicity, or gender. They have soul, dedication, and passion. Every child needs great teachers.

Politicians are the scapegoats for many of society's problems. We blame politicians for not doing enough, and then we blame them when government gets too big, because they have tried to solve problems. Money is the only solution for many politicians. It looks good for reelection when politicians can show their constituents that they brought this program or that project to their district. Money is also the most expedient solution used by many politicians. Cable news has reduced many interviews with politicians to thirty-second sound bites. Therefore, politicians who almost always are running for something must get their message out quickly, and quickly usually means something that is not thought out in depth.

Money is an important solution to the crisis in inner-city education, but it is one of the many solutions that must be initiated at the same time. The term "Good money after bad" fits well if you send lots of money to a district without changes in leadership, with commitment from the community, and with improvements in curriculum and instruction. The problems have deep roots; therefore, the solutions must be implemented with vision and depth.

Depth is a difficult word for politicians who need to run for reelection every two years. Yet depth of knowledge, insight, and purpose are necessary to attack the culture of incompetence that has festered for generations. A program here or a program there will not solve the problems. Money here or money there will not solve the problems. Politicians need to be statesmen or stateswomen and listen to all stakeholders, examine all options, and act like all children in America are their own children.

The purpose of public service for a politician should be to make the country a better place for all Americans. What better way to change the country than through improvements in education? Schools are the vehicle for a better tomorrow, because today, we are training the people who will run the country in the future. Politicians need to have some foresight to examine the issue of education in depth and over the long haul. There are no quick fixes, but there are some difficult, significant choices that all politicians can make.

Teachers are held "accountable" by many stakeholders for the failure of education in inner-city America. Since the problems are so deep and intertwined, everyone should only point a finger of blame at themselves. Often, people who want to blame teachers for all problems have fuzzy but fond memories of sitting in a classroom as a child. Everyone sat quietly in a class of forty-five children back in 1945. They never dared to talk back to their teachers, because, if a note went home, their parents would smack them before even reading it. They did their homework, and they passed. The older we are, the clearer those dreams seem to be.

The structure and types of families have changed; teachers don't receive the respect they should; and those wonderful schools are now sixty years older. That does not absolve schools from their responsibilities for the successes and failures of our education system. They have their fair share of the blame for the failures and of responsibility for the change.

All stakeholders must work together to provide every young child in America today with a fair, equal educational opportunity. The schools definitely can not do it alone in today's world. If politicians must be the public's bully pulpit for reform, then the schools must absolutely be the vehicle to drive the reforms from the drawing room to the classroom. Schools are the foot soldiers for change.

My daughter is one of the best teachers I have ever met. She and her friends face the debilitating effects of negative social forces every day. They see children coming to school in the winter without a coat. They know that some inner-city children come to school on Monday morning hungry because they had little to eat all weekend.

Schools can also be the laboratory for positive change. New curricular programs are piloted in an inner-city classroom, not in a politician's office, a business luncheon, or a university conference room. Schools must be the focal point for change, because they are also the lightning rod of the argument. All schools have choices. They can fight for their children and strive to be living schools. If they remain stagnant and static, then that is a choice as well.

All inner-city schools must analyze and prioritize the needs of their buildings, students, and staff. I am not talking about a silly, long, bureaucratic form provided by a governmental agency in order to seek state funds. I am talking about a down-to-earth document created by the people who live it every day—teachers, administrators, parents, and students. "Classroom 105 has a leak in the ceiling"; "the seventh grade needs new math textbooks"; "We need to have better curricular dialogue in the building"; and "How can we help the increasing number of Pakistani children entering the school"—these are the types of topics and concerns each school must address on their own. Administrators must be the leaders of these discussions, but if an administrator is an incompetent, political hack, then teachers on the same floor or at the same grade level could develop the dialogue. It can be done, because I have seen it done. Schools shouldn't make the choice to do nothing.

The entire school community must determine which factors it can control and which ones it must fight with the government, business, and community agencies for its fair share. The school community must maximize its positive features. An inner-city school may be located near a museum, a park, or a university. Reach out to those institutions for curricular, instructional, and volunteer assistance. Use the park as a science lab. Can the students identify the trees and bugs living right next to them? Paterson is famous for Great Falls, the second largest waterfall east of the Mississippi River. How many students have visited Great Falls? The age of the school may be an asset. Some old schools still have sliding walls, which means that teachers can team teach with large and small rooms as needed for instruction.

Teachers and administrators need to keep their rooms and schools clean. I have seen schools where children are allowed to eat, drink, and chew gum all day long. Then at the end of the day, the last class just throws all the junk out of their desks onto the floor for the janitors to sweep and clean. Yuck! When those children work as adults someday, will they be allowed to act that way with their office desks? Maybe that is one reason why so many students can't keep good jobs when they are older. It is the parents' responsibility to make sure their children keep their rooms clean at home, so they have some experience to keep their classroom clean and neat.

If I walk into any classroom, there should be evidence that children are working in that room. Teachers should hang students' work prominently throughout the room. Bright colors will help erase dingy corridors in the building or in the neighborhood. Students should create their own bulletin boards. Ownership and empowerment will carry over into their work at home and at school.

Teachers should demand that their rooms be cleaned every night. There is no excuse for everyone in the building not to be doing their assigned jobs. If any stakeholder accepts the culture of incompetence, then we have made the choice to perpetuate atrocious conditions in the school. Rooms should be swept, garbage emptied, and boards washed. Can we expect children to work hard in a room that has not been cleaned in days? Again, it is an example of "They don't care about me, why should I care about me?"

Newspapers and paperwork can make a classroom and school look chaotic and sloppy if they are allowed to be left on floors or windowsills. Every school should have a recycling program for paper and bottles. Is there a better way to teach responsibility and citizenship? Is there any better way for a school to prove that it wants to be a living school than with examples of building a better environment for tomorrow? Maybe schools can use the money from the recycling program to plant flowers or plants in or outside the school. Teachers and administrators need to make the choice to have their school live.

Epilogue

Is It Brauhway or Broadway?

Education is simple yet profound. Parents literally or figuratively walk their prize children to the schoolhouse door every September, and say essentially, "Here. They are yours for the next year. Treat them with the same kindness and respect that I do, and teach them to be better people and citizens. Teach them about our great country and its promise of equality and opportunity. Teach them to get along with one another and to judge people by the content of their character and not the color of their skin. Teach them to be responsible yet compassionate adults."

I was blessed to become a grandpa a few years ago, and the feeling is indescribable. If you are a grandpa, or hope to be one someday, think about the children in dilapidated schools with old books. Think about them walking home through even more dilapidated streets to get to a home where someone may or may not be there to care for and love them. If we are all our brothers' keepers, then, in a real sense, we are all someone's grandpa or grandma. We do have a social, moral, and ethical responsibility to one another, especially to those who can't fend for themselves. Be a grandpa or grandma to someone who needs you. Be a great American.

All Americans can use the bully pulpit to demand responsibility from all the stakeholders toward the education of children. It is wrong for children to make babies, and we need to tell teenagers that. It is wrong for parents not to know where their children are or for parents to allow them to walk the streets at all hours of the day and night. Politicians, clergy, parents, and teachers need to make those speeches.

Teachers must be professionals at all times and reform themselves when necessary. They must revile the Donut Dans in their teacher lounges as pariahs rather than as prophets. Teachers need to be compensated for quality work, but they must recognize that, if salaries do increase substantially, it is their responsibility to keep their professional houses clean. No stakeholder should accept the culture of incompetence, but teachers must be at the front of the line of protest. They work with the children every day and see the waste of human lives each year.

Politicians must be the vehicle that demands accountability and cooperation from all stakeholders responsible for the education of our future adult citizens. They are representatives of Americans and are, therefore, are also responsible to all stakeholders. If inner-city education is to be changed, then all stakeholders must be aligned and fighting the same fight.

Teachers need to stand up for their students. They must not accept the status quo. They need to be an advocate for their profession—it is a noble, righteous one. They should not prostitute their teaching certificates to politicians, the streets, or expediency. Teachers need to choose the road less traveled and fight for the children who do not have the power to fight for themselves.

Teaching is a unique profession filled with hope and despair. There were many stories of frustration in this book, but I believe I balanced them with examples of hope and joy. If someone loves children and believes in their abilities, that person should become a teacher and feel the ecstasy. Hope does spring eternal as long as there are new generations of young teachers willing to put their courage and enthusiasm on the line for the neediest of children.

When I was a supervisor of social studies classes, I moved around the city on a daily basis. I met many former students who still lived and worked in the community. I almost ran into two lovely former students, who were driving their car in the downtown area. They stopped short and yelled, "Mr. C, we need directions." They had always been hardworking, pleasant, young ladies in school, and I was pleased to see that they had retained that charm. I gave them directions, which included a turn on Broadway. They roared hysterically, and I asked them what was wrong?

Still laughing, they exclaimed, "Mr. C, there's no *D* in Brauhway."

I hope and pray that those two women will maintain their innocence and charm for their entire lives. Teachers just have to love children and want to work with them to improve their lives. That is the joy and hope of education.

When I was still teaching in the performing arts high school, there was a move toward site-based management and budgeting. I was a member of a committee to plan for the following school year. One teacher wondered how many students in our performing arts school had ever been to Broadway to see a hit play. We decided to raise money and send our children to Broadway. We chose our play, *Bring in 'Da Noise, Bring in 'Da Funk*, did some additional begging for funds, and one day, sent three hundred students, faculty, and community members to Broadway on seven buses.

Since it was an expensive trip, we wanted to make a full day out of it. That morning each major teacher—there were seven majors that students could audition in for acceptance into the school—selected a school or landmark in Manhattan that was relevant to the students' future professions. All seven buses were to descend on Times Square for lunch and a walk to the theater.

Needless to say, I was very nervous. Would the students all get to eat and arrive at the theater on time? But as my bus entered Times Square, I could count the other six arriving from different directions. We all had had time to eat and form a long line outside the theater.

It was a spectacular day, and one that those aspiring artists and performers would never forget. There was enough joy, hope, and enthusiasm for the world coming from those buses on the way home from the theater. That's what makes the broken school windows, bad heat, and old books bearable.

I believe a task force on education should be established by the president of the United States and funded by Congress. That task force should include representatives of all stakeholders in the future of our educational system, specifically the inner cities. A plan with the significance and scope of the Marshall Plan after World War II must be created and funded. The plan must be supported by all Americans with the same enthusiasm as when we backed the trips to the moon in the sixties. Poverty, poor health and nutrition, low expectations, old facilities, single-parent families, racism, politics, and many more issues must all be open to discussion.

Let's not think about the quick fix, because there is none. Let's not decide on singular choices of money or accountability, responsibility or support. Tackle all problems and solutions simultaneously.

As I have said repeatedly, the problems facing inner-city schools today are interwoven like a spider's web. Throw money or time at just one, and the other problems will entangle and destroy any positive gains. We must address every problem that faces the education of young, poor children with equal vigor.

Let's not think about which group likes or distrusts what group. Let's leave our personal issues, prejudices, and hatred at home and think about this generation of young American children entering school. Everything needs to be pulled out from under the rug, and everything must be put on the table. Let's stop pointing fingers at one another and join those fingers with other people who believe in the promise of America as stated in our Declaration of Independence. If we can't prepare our children for the future, what is our reason for existence as a nation? Let's break away from the culture of incompetence by making intelligent choices aimed at educating all children in America equally and fairly.

God bless all parents who still believe that the American Dream can be achieved through a quality education. God bless all teachers who work long hours and buy chalk and markers out of their own meager salaries, because they believe that all children can learn. God bless community and business members who believe that they have a responsibility to the common good. Finally, God bless all children who fight monsters in the streets every day to learn algebra, physics, and the history of this great country. Especially, God bless the children of Paterson, New Jersey.

Breinigsville, PA USA
23 December 2009
229744BV00001B/43/P